CATSKILL TRAILS

A Ranger's Guide to the High Peaks

BOOK ONE: THE NORTHERN CATSKILLS

Edward G. Henry

BLACK·DOME

Black Dome Press Corp.
1011 Route 296
Hensonville, New York 12439
Tel: (518) 734-6357
Fax: (518) 734-5802
www.blackdomepress.com

Published by
Black Dome Press Corp.
1011 Route 296
Hensonville, New York 12439
www.blackdomepress.com
Tel: (518) 734-6357 Fax: (518) 734-5802

Library of Congress Cataloging-in-Publication Data:

Henry, Edward G.
    Catskill trails: a ranger's guide to the high peaks/by Edward G. Henry.
      p. cm.
    Contents: bk. 1. The northern Catskills
    ISBN 1-883789-22-2 (trade paper)
    1. Hiking--New York (State)--Catskill Mountains--Guidebooks. 2. Trails
    --New York (State)--Catskill Mountains--Guidebooks. 3. Catskill
    Mountains (N.Y.)--Guidebooks.

    GV199.42.N652 C373 2000

                                            00-026162

Outdoor recreational activities are by their very nature potentially hazardous and contain risk. Please see CAUTION, pg. 4.

The maps in this book were created using TOPO! Interactive Maps from Wildflower Productions. To learn more about digital map products from Wildflower, please visit www.topo.com or call 415.558.8700

Photos by Edward G. Henry

Design by Carol Clement, Artemisia, Inc.
Printed in the USA

10   9   8   7

To my Grandfathers

CAUTION

Outdoor recreation activities are by their very nature potentially hazardous and contain risk. All participants in such activities must assume the responsibility for their own actions and safety. The outdoors are forever changing. No book can replace good judgment. The author and the publisher cannot be held responsible for inaccuracies, errors or omissions or for changes in the details in this publication or for the consequences of any reliance on the information contained herein or for the safety of people in the outdoors.

HIKING RULES AND GUIDELINES

1. Dress appropriately—cotton clothing and sneakers are the number one cause of illness and injury leading to emergency evacuation.
2. Be prepared—have a first aid kit, whistle, flashlight, matches, small tarp, extra high-energy food, and water.
3. Sign in and out at trail registers.
4. Wear and use appropriate snow gear when the trails are snow-covered.
5. Make sure all campsites are more than 150 feet from a trail or water, or in a designated site.
6. Treat all water before drinking—use chemicals, a filter, or boil for more than two minutes.
7. When camping, hang all food and garbage from a tree at least 50 feet from camp, 15 feet or more above the ground, and 8 feet or more from tree trunks and limbs.
8. Use pre-existing fire rings when possible. Make sure all fires are completely extinguished before breaking camp.
9. Camping permits are needed for groups of 10 or more people, or for one or more people staying in the same place for more than three consecutive nights.
10. Camping and fires are prohibited above 3500 feet between March 22 and December 20 of each year.

And remember: if you carry it in, carry it out!

ACKNOWLEDGMENTS

First of all, I want to thank all my friends who accompanied me on many of my Catskill hikes, especially Shawn Keizer and John Butnor whose companionship on the trail and throughout my life has always been welcomed and enjoyed. Reggie Carlson, Mike Olexa, Billy Kuhne, and a host of others also played a role in joining me on the trails, as reviewers of this book, and as friends and supporters that I always will appreciate, and always have.

The catalyst for this book trails back to Labor Day of 1989 when my friend Sue Ives invited me to go camping in Woodland Valley. Late on that Friday afternoon, she recommended that we hike Wittenberg Mountain. It was a tough hike, but once we crested the peak and the trees parted to reveal the Ashokan Reservoir, eastern Catskills, Hudson Valley, and points east, my eyes and my soul were filled with a new wonder. From that point on, this book was a certainty. Thank you, Sue.

From the professional arena I want to thank all the people who helped bring the book to fruition. Debbie Allen and Steve Hoare at Black Dome Press have been wonderful to work with and very gentle with me. I also want to acknowledge the efforts of Patricia H. Davis, Matina Billias and Doris West Brooks whose experience with words and the Catskills helped polish this work in ways that only their experience and talents could. Carol Clement brought an expertise and efficiency to the production of this book that only a graphic designer who is also a licensed hiking guide could offer. (She and her partners are often found on these very trails guiding for their tour company, High Land Flings Footloose Holidays.)

I thank Dr. Michael Kudish, whose work and occasional correspondence has been of tremendous help to me in learning about the Catskills and its forests. In addition, I want to express how pleased I was to have the editorial and technical help of Jack Sencabaugh. We may be from a different generation, but we share many of the same

5

loves. Having someone of his caliber associated with my work is, indeed, a pleasure.

I also wish to thank my parents—my Mother for her reviewing and editing skills, and my Father for getting me started with photography, the skill that first got me interested in exploring the Catskill Mountains and the rest of the world.

And to my wife Kerry—I must thank you for putting up with my infatuation with the Catskills and for giving me the time I needed to write this book. Without your love and support an accomplishment such as this could not be so sweet.

FOREWORD

Ed Henry is a native of the Catskills, has a forestry degree and has worked for years in National Parks. I'm a forester, too, but of an earlier generation. We've never met, yet we seem to share the same love of wild lands that the Catskill Mountains—especially that part of the mountains within the New York State Forest Preserve—exemplify.

I worked in all of the territory in the northern Catskills of which Henry writes. He describes it so well that his narrative transported me back to those magical forests and mountains. As I read, I could once again see those magnificent views, feel the trail beneath my feet, hear the wind in the trees and smell the fresh scent of spruce needles.

I was reminded of the work of the poet Bliss Carman, who wrote often of the Catskills in the early 1900s. In his poem, "The Cry of the Hillborn," he penned these words:

> I am homesick for the mountains—
> My heroic mother hills—
> And the longing that is on me
> No solace ever stills.
>
> I would climb to brooding summits
> With their old untarnished dreams,
> Cool my heart in forest shadows
> To the lull of falling streams.

With *Catskill Trails*, Ed Henry has written a unique and very readable hiking book. Its uniqueness, its difference from other such books, lies in its strong emphasis on the geology of the mountains, the description of forest vegetation and how it changes as the hikes progress, and the almost poetic invocation of scenes along the way.

Many users of the Catskill trail system hike simply for exercise and to get from point A to point B to get "the view"; they see little along the way. Henry believes that the more the hiker observes and learns and understands, the more appreciative the hiker will be of the awe-inspiring complexity of nature. That appreciation should, in turn, lead to a deeper respect for nature and a keener sense of one's own place within it.

Aldo Leopold (another forester) once wrote in his *Sand County Almanac* about the reason for building hiking trails. The goal, he wrote, is "... not one of building trails into lovely country, but of building receptivity into the yet unloving human mind." Henry's descriptive insights can help build that receptivity.

Jack Sencabaugh
Catskill, New York
March 1, 2000

Preface

To experience the Catskill Mountains through exploration creates a life-long bond. This book uses hiking trails throughout the Catskills as guides to the region's natural history. Each mountain, ridgetop, waterfall, and clove tells its own natural story.

Through photos, personal experiences, and written descriptions, the Catskills' ecology, history, and spirit unfolds. Beautiful mountain vistas, breathtaking waterfalls, and rugged trails become opportunities to discover the forces shaping nature. Silent bedrock cliffs, light summer breezes caressing a stand of sugar maple, and babbling brooks are part of the experience.

Natural history is an open field. In this book's examination of the Catskills' natural history, it employs forest ecology, geology, meteorology, wildlife biology, geography, economics, and history to reveal a fuller picture of the Catskill Mountains and the interconnected forces that shaped them.

For convenience and continuity, this book divides the Catskills geographically. The southern and western Catskills, a series of low, rounded hills are not covered here. This book concentrates on areas with peaks above 3,500 feet. Delineated by glacial features, the Catskills' high peaks divide into a northern and southern half. This book, the first of a two-volume set, covers the northern Catskills. In the 1800s, people reinforced this split when they referred to the southern Catskills as the Shandaken Mountains. Within each half, closely related peaks make additional groupings. Many shared characteristics, however, cross these artificial boundaries, the result of arbitrary, human decisions. The mountains are the mountains; they do not divide into neat groups, nor do they heed man's classifications.

Although this work stands alone, it is only a starting place. The Catskills await anyone wishing to explore its slopes. The list of traveled routes is designed to serve as an introduction to further explorations.

I'm happy you've decided to join me in exploring the Catskills. I'm not sure exactly where we'll be going today, for that's up to you, and the Catskills offer many choices. Perhaps we'll visit the summit of Roundtop Mountain, one of my favorites. There is no trail to the top, but it is easy to get there. We'll climb through a maturing northern hardwood forest, stems of sugar maple, American beech, yellow birch, and black cherry shading the steep slopes and ledges. Silvery flashes of sunlight dance on the forest floor, a gentle breeze changing the kaleidoscope pattern of light and dark. Hard, gray Hamilton sandstones force the mountain upward. At about 3,100 feet we pass the circular snowmobile trail. The level ledge supporting it is more mud than anything else, the glacially-gouged rock shelf unable to drain.

Soon the forest changes, with paper birch and red spruce replacing beech and sugar maple. The slope steepens, and the trees become smaller. Mountain maple, mountain-ash, hobblebush, and yellow birch become the dominant tree species. The soil is shallow, almost black, the steep slopes unable to hold soil or large trees. Wooden limbs litter the ground along with a host of assorted boulders. Then the mountain levels and we're on the summit, a mix of forest and field. Fresh, sweet blueberries provide a refreshing snack. Views open to the east and west. To the east looms Kaaterskill High Peak, its dome rising another 125 feet above Roundtop. Kaaterskill High Peak falls to the north and south into two steep valleys, or cloves, some of the most rugged country in the eastern United States. Farther east is the gentle blanket of the Hudson Valley. A wide blue ribbon, the Hudson River, slowly flows south. The scene is one for the ages, painted by landscape artists of the late 19th century, and enjoyed by modern day adventurers as well.

This volume only covers the Catskills' northern half, the area considered "the Catskills" in the early and mid-1800s when the mountains to the south and west, including Slide Mountain, were called the

Shandaken Mountains. While the mountains are all of one origin and history, the split makes a distinct break between the northern and southern halves of the Catskills. Starting at the southern wall of Platte Clove and the southern slopes along Devil's Path, the line continues to the southern wall of Spruceton Valley. Following Route 42 south, the line then meets with the Esopus Valley and heads west, cresting the Hudson-Delaware divide north of Belleayre Mountain. The mountains north of this line, including Hunter and the Blackheads, the second-fifth highest Catskill summits, are the subject of this volume. The southern Catskills are the subject of Book II.

Most mountainous areas have an elevation status that defines its high peaks. In the Catskills, this number is 3,500 feet. This book includes all the peaks above this "magic" number, plus other, lower peaks and areas with significant vistas or other landmarks. Among these places are the Catskill's finest waterfalls and cloves. (Cloves are steep, rocky valleys, often inaccessible by car, that can climb 2,000 feet or more in elevation in less than a mile.)

The routes to each peak were chosen either because they were the shortest route to the peak or main destination, or because there was something else special along the way that makes taking a longer route worthwhile. Some of the hikes are loops since it is always more fun and interesting to cover new ground than to backtrack, even if it takes a little longer. In some cases, the shortest route entails some very steep slopes, but the challenge and physical rewards of keeping in shape make the tough hikes worthwhile. A few of the routes I use are off-trail and require additional safety awareness. Although some of the routes skirt private land, you should not enter posted land without prior permission; none of the hikes listed here encourage nor require trespass. The routes I used to write this book, along with mile notes, are listed in the appendix.

The Catskills are a special place. As I've traveled and explored the Catskill Mountains, I've come to love them and learn from them. The mountains and their stories have become a part of my fabric. Putting this information into a book was almost second nature.

Even though I grew up at the mountains' edge, I did not become attached to the peaks until my sophomore year in college. One weekend, a friend asked me to go camping at Woodland Valley. We hiked to Wittenberg and Giant Ledge. The views were incredible! The rounded mountains, the soft green forests, the sapphire blue of the Ashokan Reservoir, and the distant horizon in Vermont, Massachusetts, and Connecticut captured my imagination and soul. I was hooked. I started hiking all the peaks and photographing all the views. I used topographic maps to learn the names and shapes of all the mountains. Soon I was putting knowledge I learned in school to work interpreting the mountains.

And so I experienced the deep roar and cool spray of Kaaterskill Falls, stiff breezes atop Wittenberg Mountain while taking in its incredible vista, and peaceful evenings pondering the pastel pinks, purples, and oranges of a sunset from the Ashokan Reservoir's eastern shore. Each of these scenes is only a small facet of the Catskill Mountain gemstone. I started writing about my experiences, and these efforts led to this book.

While my formal training is in forest ecology and my career is in professional conservation, I use subjects ranging from geology to economics to reveal the Catskill Mountain story. I hope throughout the book you will no longer walk along anonymous trails and see a series of impersonal hills and waterfalls; rather, I hope you will look into the forest and envision past logging and the process of succession, get to know the tree species and wildlife, touch the icy waters of a trout stream, smell the honeyed air of spring, taste the tartness of sheep sorrel, and see the remnants and signs of the past ice age. Perhaps you will be able to imagine the Catskills buried in a sea of ice with the exception of Slide Mountain's summit, its peak a lone beacon among the expanse of dirty ice. My hope is that this book can help you experience the mountains in a way more personal and inspirational than just following a bunch of trail signs could ever be, and that you will experience the Catskills as a natural historian rather than a tourist.

Kaaterskill Falls

Hiking a mountain peak is a three-dimensional experience, but time, the fourth dimension, is often ignored. With a trained eye, you may see the Catskills not just as they are in the present, but as they looked in the past, and, perhaps, how they will appear in the future. The story of the Catskills is more than 500 million years old, but as easy to read as picking up a rock or looking at a rounded mountaintop. By exploring the Catskills through time, you will experience the rise and fall of great mountain ranges, ice ages, changing forests, and man's economic activity.

There are a few things I cannot stress enough when you are exploring the Catskills. First, wear appropriate footwear. If your feet are not happy, you will not be happy, no matter how great the view. Second, always have enough water for your trip. Whether you carry it in, use a filter, or chemically treat your water, make sure you have enough. Do not drink untreated water, as it can have *Giardia*, a disease that will turn your digestive system inside out for months. Third, bring a map and compass along with you. It's always good to have an idea of where you are in the mountains, and it will help you maintain a sense of direction. As global positioning satellite units (often referred to as GPS units) become more affordable and reliable, they will become another option for remaining oriented in the forest. Used properly, a GPS makes it almost impossible to get lost. Some would even call using a GPS "cheating." In addition, carry a small first aid kit and dress for the weather.

The Catskill Mountains are part of an ongoing process. Mother Nature never finishes her landscapes, but she works on a time scale much longer than a human lifespan. We may never see the mountains as any different than they look today, but we do play a role in their current appearance. Perhaps the most disturbing thing visitors do is litter. Whether a soda can a quarter-mile from the trailhead, or a 40-year-old candy wrapper along the top ridge of a trail-less mountain peak, it sends the message, "I don't care." While most people do not litter, neither do most of us pick up litter left by others. If there is one favor I would ask as you explore the Catskills, it is to please try and leave the place a little cleaner than you found it. If we all did that, man's garbage would not escort us to most of the mountaintops, and all those little pieces of litter would not slap the concept of wilderness in the face.

The Catskills' story is a long and complex tale, but it is not too hard to follow if you know what to look for in the landscape. I have attempted to bring to you as much of this story as possible, and give you the ability to look deeper for yourself. And maybe, if I've done a good job, I'll be able to transplant to you a little bit of my love for the Catskills.

On Huntersfield, looking south at Slide, Northdome, Sherill and Balsam

TABLE OF CONTENTS

An Introduction to the Catskills

The Catskill Mountains rise west of the Hudson River in southeastern New York, roughly 100 miles north-northwest of New York City. The highest peaks are in Ulster and Greene Counties. Lower mountains associated with the Catskills stretch into Delaware, Sullivan, and Schoharie Counties. Elevations of the Catskills' 50 highest summits range from 3,400 to 4,180 feet. The highest peaks, those above 3,500 feet, form the Catskill High Peaks, and are the basis for the Catskill 3500 Club; club membership requires hiking all of these peaks.

In the eastern Catskills, a spruce-fir forest dominates elevations above 3,300 feet. Most western summits support balsam fir forests or upper hardwoods. Northern hardwoods, mainly sugar maple, beech, and yellow birch, cover the middle and lower slopes. Hemlock forests line most stream courses. The lowland valleys often contain mixed hardwood species, while pine-oak forests grace the dry, exposed ridges.

The Catskills have a cool, moist climate characterized by mild summers and cold winters. Mean average temperature at 3,000 feet is 38F degrees: 61F degrees in July, and 14F degrees in January. The growing season lasts about 120 days. The high summits in the moister eastern Catskills receive about 65 inches of annual precipitation. Drier western summits get about 50 inches. Slide Mountain, the wettest peak, receives 70 inches each year. Snow accounts for 20 percent of annual precipitation, an average of 140 inches.

Set 100 miles north and west of the Atlantic Ocean, the ocean does not influence local temperature; however, as ocean moisture moves inland and rises, orographic (mountain influenced) precipitation arises. Precipitation in the eastern and southern Catskills is up to a third greater than surrounding valleys. Orographic lifting also influences temperature, producing a 3-5F degree change for each 1,000 feet. The city of Kingston, at sea level on the Hudson River, averages 16F degrees warmer than Slide Mountain's summit.

Wind is another major factor in the Catskills' upper elevations. Mountain and valley breezes develop on most sunny days. Prevailing winds are from the west. The mountains enhance winds associated with fronts and storms. Gusts of 40 miles per hour and higher are common.

The first white men to see the Catskills were the crew on Henry Hudson's ship, *Half Moon*, in September of 1609. At that time, Indian tribes living between the river and the Catskill Mountains were mainly of the Minnisink and Delaware tribes. To the north were the Mohawks, fearsome warriors of the Iroquois Confederacy. Indians generally avoided the Catskills, preferring the warmer climates of the surrounding valleys, but summer hunting parties frequented the mountains.

Early European settlement was Dutch, an influence remaining through place names and spellings. Many streams retain the Dutch suffix of "kill." The name Catskill may derive from the Dutch for "wildcat stream." Bobcats, and some people claim mountain lions as well, still roam the mountains. The Catskills were also called the Blue or Blew Mountains, due to their color and harsh weather.

The fertile, mild climate of the Hudson Valley attracted many settlers. Huge estates and small farmsteads lined both riverbanks. While many had beautiful views of the Catskills, few settlers did more than ponder that beauty from the civilized valleys.

Conflicts in the mid-1660s led to English occupation and rule, but life changed little for the Dutch settlers, and few troubles arose. Like the Dutch, the English discouraged westward expansion, yet even without governmental policy Europeans shunned the Catskills, associating the foreboding mountains with evil spirits. Settlers spread into the valleys slowly, but it was not until logging concerns invaded the Catskills that society lost this irrational fear.

Among the strongest events discouraging settlement was a famous land deal, the Hardenburgh Patent. A grant of 2 million acres to Johannis Hardenburgh in 1708 kept the Catskills closed to settlement, and opened legal battles lasting into the 20th century. The grant included most of what is now Ulster, Greene, Sullivan, and Delaware Counties. Eventually, the Livingstons and other prominent families bought into the land grant.

As more and more people came to the Hudson Valley, some settlers began to move into the mountains to make a new life and find greater freedom. But farming the Catskills was difficult. The land, covered with only a thin soil, did not retain fertility. Bound to the land through long-term contracts, local residents lived a difficult and poor life. Few people had the freedom to leave or to explore the mountains.

Along with agriculture, forestry became a major industry. Throughout the mid-1800s, tanneries cut the Catskills' mighty hemlock stands for their bark, a source of tannin, which was used in leather production. Raw hides came to the Catskills from as far away as Argentina. Within a few decades, the Catskill forests lay in ruin. Without the hemlocks, the tanning industry collapsed and the region's prosperity ended. Until the mid-1900s, the Catskills would be socio-economically considered part of Appalachia.

The Catskills' only recognized natural resources were building stone and trees. Stripped of their timber, economic ruin characterized the Catskill Mountains in the late 1800s. Only tourism remained viable, and it declined beginning in the early 1900s. Time and opportunity drew people away and, eventually, the sparsely settled region provided a better livelihood for those remaining. In 1885, New York State formed the Catskill State Park from the abandoned and abused mountains, and as New York City grew, the Catskills' clean water became a major natural resource, a fact not lost to politicians and businessmen when considering the Park's creation.

Today, the Catskill State Park encompasses more than 700,000 acres, a third directly stewarded by New York State. Much of the land is set aside by the New York State Constitution as "forever wild." Most of the high peaks lie within the publicly-owned Park. The preserved and recovering lands provide sanctuary, wilderness, and adventure for visitors and residents. Despite debates over the role of government in land ownership and use, the rejuvenated Catskills are a natural resource whose current ecological value is beyond question. To explore the Catskills is to experience the beauty, diversity, and abundance thriving in the mountains.

Haines Falls

A Brief Geologic History
of the Catskill Mountains

The Catskills are one-sided mountains. Many appear cast from the same mold. A steep eastern front builds to a summit, followed by a gentle western slope. Northern slopes have fewer side ridges than southern faces. Despite the passage of 380 million years since their formation, the Catskills' strata display similar physical characteristics that evolved under shared environmental conditions.

On a smaller scale, individual mountains display distinctive characteristics as ice, water, and wind eroded each peak differently. Mountains appearing identical from one side reveal distinctive subtleties from other perspectives. A rounded slope out of place, a shoulder dipping at a different angle, a deeper notch, or a steeper summit—each individualizes the mountains.

Geographically part of the Appalachians, the Catskills are the highest section of the Allegheny Plateau. The uplifted plateau evolved into mountains as erosion dissected the high, level surface. Running west of the Appalachians and parallel to them, this eroded plateau runs from New York to Tennessee. Other well-known regions of the Allegheny Plateau include Pennsylvania's Pocono Mountains and the Cumberland Plateau in Kentucky and Tennessee.

The Appalachian Mountains parallel North America's east coast, constantly struggling against erosion. Stretching from Maine to Alabama within the United States, these quiet, picturesque mountains reveal few clues to their rugged past. The highest point remaining in the North American Appalachians is North Carolina's Mount Mitchell at 6,684 feet above sea level.

The Appalachians extend far beyond the United States. They cross into Canada as the Shuckstacks before they slide into the Atlantic Ocean. When the ocean formed, its waters split the great mountain chain. The range emerges from the Atlantic as Scotland's Caledonian Mountains. They rise again from the Baltic Sea as Norway's fjords and mountains. The chain's highest peak is Norway's Mount Goldhopiggen at 8,097 feet above sea level.

The Catskills' geologic history began long before the formation of its rocks. Events of the past 1.1 billion years created complex geologic structures below the area's surface strata. Entire mountain chains rose and eroded on the land currently topped by the Catskills. Seas lapped against sandy beaches and great fern forests thrived on coastal plains. The Catskills' exposed Devonian sandstones and shales sit atop these rocks. Their perseverance, or lack of it, influenced the Catskills' geologic evolution.

North America is more than one billion years old. As geologic eras passed, North America grew, condensed, and changed. As it drifted, its orientation also changed. While continental positions in this book are relative to their current locations, keep in mind that North America wandered during the past billion years. At the time of the Appalachian Orogeny (mountain building event), 290 million years ago, North America's east coast sat along the equator.

North America's Precambrian history is poorly understood. The rock record reveals more questions than it answers. Beyond the creation of the region's basement rock, few events that old relate to the Catskills.

The Taconic Orogeny is the first well-defined event affecting the Catskills. The Taconic Mountains lifted 450 million years ago as North America and Northern Europe (called Baltica) collided. Together, these land masses formed the Old Red Sandstone Continent. Few features remain from these ancient mountains. Rivers eroded the range particle by particle, filling a basin to the west. Although the mountains no longer exist, the river systems solidified into the Queenston Delta. These rocks, buried beneath the Catskills, surface from western New York to Ohio. Today, the Taconic Mountains' stumps are the Taconic Hills in eastern New York and the Berkshires in western New England. From many Catskill summits, these hills define the eastern horizon.

Once the Earth's forces settled, the Taconics stopped lifting and began to erode. At this time, Gondwana, which included southern Europe, Florida, Africa, and South America, pushed toward the Old Red Sandstone Continent. An ocean, the Iapetus, separated the two land masses. Britain and a volcanic island chain, Avalon, split the Iapetus Ocean into eastern and western halves.

With the Taconics eroding, an inland sea invaded eastern North America. Corals thrived in these shallow tropical waters. Thick, calcium-rich layers covered the Queenston Delta while it began its transition to rock. The corals that lived during the Ordovician period formed limestone, and some evolved into dolomite. These calcareous rocks lie beneath the Catskills' sandstones and shales. They surface north and east of the mountains in the Hudson, Mohawk, Schoharie, Esopus, and Wallkill Valleys. A few thin layers of limestone mix with the Catskills' lower strata. Plant species requiring high calcium levels thrive near these layers.

The sediments forming the Catskills' strata originated from an extinct mountain chain. Born in the Silurian Era 380 million years ago, the Acadian Mountains formed as Avalon and North America collided. Set along North America's east coast, the Acadian Mountains rose 25,000 feet above sea level. Their peaks danced with the clouds. At this time the British Isles melded with Baltica, an event that closed the eastern Iapetus Ocean.

Millions of years passed. During the Devonian Period the western Iapetus contracted as Gondwana (formed of a merged southern Europe, South America, and Africa) moved toward North America and Baltica. As the Acadian Mountains eroded, sediments migrated into a shallow inland sea. As its basin filled, its shores retreated westward. A progression of size-sorted sediments formed, the clays and silts traveling farther than the sands. The sands often dropped from the rivers as they entered their deltas. Cross-bedding patterns preserved in the Catskills' sandstones reflect this deposition.

As the inland sea evaporated and retreated, it left a salt layer. This layer sits beneath the Catskills' strata. Since salts flow under high pressure, they form weak rock, shifting and cracking rocks above them. At the surface, these movements result in jointing—a major feature of Catskill sandstones.

A series of rivers transported the eroding Acadian Mountains to the sea. Sediment loads accumulated as waters slowed in lowland areas.

Together, these sediments form the Catskill Clastic Wedge, better known as the Catskill Delta. The landscape resembled America's Gulf Coast. After 50 million years, the Acadian Mountains evolved into a peneplain (flat surface). Sedimentary rocks derived from these mountains stretch from the Catskills' eastern escarpment to the Pennsylvania-Ohio border.

Sediments from the Acadian Mountains accumulated as 15,000 feet of sand, silt, and clay. Thickest near the mountains' base, these sediments covered the future Hudson Valley (there was no Hudson River until 75 million years ago) and the Taconics' stumps.

The Devonian and Mississippian Periods passed, and the Iapetus Ocean began to close. Gondwana and the Old Red Sandstone Continent drifted together. Friction built, and volcanoes erupted in the shrinking ocean forming an archipelago off North America's east coast. The island chain resembled Japan. All the while, North America and Africa continued on a collision course, dooming the young islands trapped between them. The Iapetus Ocean perished when North America and Africa collided. This event also bonded northern and southern Europe. Florida merged with North America.

When the Appalachian Orogeny began 290 million years ago, it marked the birth of the super-continent Pangea. The world's greatest mountain range, the Appalachians, covered eastern North America and northern Europe. Ever since, some remnant of these mountains has remained along North America's east coast.

During this mountain-building event, hundreds of miles of rock in eastern North America bent, folded, and faulted. In contrast with these deformed rocks, including the neighboring Shawangunks, the Catskill Delta did not buckle. Removed from the collision, the delta rose 7,500 feet. No horizontal deformation occurred. The Acadian Mountains' sediments, now hardened into rock, became the template for the Catskill Plateau.

In time, the Earth's forces split Pangea, and a new ocean formed. Europe and Africa retreated from North America and created the Atlantic Ocean. Centered on the Mid-Atlantic Ridge, this ocean continues to expand as it pushes on adjoining continental plates.

The Earth heaved and buckled when the Appalachians formed, yet erosion's ever-present forces immediately began removing the land. Water, wind, and ice weathered the rock, forming steep slopes, sharp ravines and deep valleys. The sediment-laden waters gathered into nameless rivers, most long extinct, and descended toward the precursors of the Atlantic Ocean and Gulf of Mexico.

Differential erosion sculpted this plateau into mountains. Unlike most mountains that form from faulted and folded rocks, the Catskills eroded from a plateau into peaks, valleys, and gorges. More than 7,500 feet of sediments compose the Catskills. Half lie below sea level, and sediment depth decreases to the west. Most sediments eroded from the Catskills flow into the Hudson River; all enter the Atlantic Ocean. Ice ages rounded the peaks and widened the valleys. Steep cloves and tumbling waterfalls result.

The Catskills abruptly end at their eastern escarpment. No trace of the Catskill Delta remains east of this point. The Hudson Valley occupies the gap, but geologists do not know if the Hudson River, which is only 75 million years old, was around to remove the sediments. The Catskills' disappearing sediments remain a geologic mystery.

The highest point remaining on this ancient plateau is 4,180-foot Slide Mountain. Most of the Catskill summits reach 3,400-3,800 feet. Areas with weaker rocks eroded faster, becoming the valleys. The erosion continues, and streams constantly transport sediments released by physical and chemical weathering. Rock slides move material downslope, scarring the landscape. In the early 1820s, a massive 1,200-foot landslide reworked Slide Mountain's northeastern face, naming the mountain in the process. Other large slides affected Wittenberg, Blackhead, Sugarloaf, and Friday Mountains.

A hard, erosion-resistant conglomerate called Catskill Puddingstone caps many of the Catskills' summits. As the current mountaintop bedrock, it shows signs of heavy erosion. Studded with rounded quartz pebbles from the Acadian Mountains, it erodes into a pebble-filled gravel. Other peaks have a hard, coarse-grained sandstone. Beneath these caprocks are the Hamilton and Oneonta formations. Kaaterskill Falls reveals the junction between these two rock types. Throughout the Catskills, resistant Hamilton sandstones support ridges, while shales erode into deep valleys.

Besides stream, water, and wind erosion, glaciation played a role in shaping the Catskills. Although many ice sheets buried and altered the region, only the most recent advances show signs of passage. The Wisconsin Ice Sheet moved south 100,000 years ago, obliterating past signs of glaciation. This continental ice sheet culminated 22,000 years ago during a surge known as the Woodfordian advance. Barely covering the Catskills, this advance may not have buried Slide Mountain's summit. Slide's isolated peak, a nanatak, would have protruded as a lonely rock beacon among a sea of ice.

As the Wisconsin Ice Sheet spread into New York, it faced two major barriers: the Adirondack and Catskill Mountains. The two ranges funneled the ice into adjoining lowlands. Ice plowed through the Champlain, Hudson, and Mohawk Valleys. It moved into the Catskills slowly. The mountains diverted the main ice tongue into the Mid-Hudson Valley. A smaller tongue penetrated the mountains via the Schoharie Valley. Moving south and east through the Schoharie and its tributaries, it reached the escarpment wall's backside. The 3,000-foot wall prevented the ice from merging with the Hudson Valley lobe.

Ice from the Hudson Valley scoured Kaaterskill and Platte Cloves. Eventually, it spilled over the cloves' walls, joining ice from the Schoharie Valley. Heavily eroded by ice, the northern Catskills reflect their glaciated past. While the ice built in the cloves, small ice tongues pushed though the Devil's Path notches: Jimmy Dolan Notch, Pecoy Notch, Mink Hollow, and Stony Clove.

The southeastern Catskills remained free of ice for longer periods. After the Woodfordian surge, lesser glacial episodes invaded the northern and eastern Catskills. The Wagon Wheel advance, occurring 17,000 years ago, penetrated well into the Esopus Valley to lap against the central high peaks. A final glacial onslaught, the Grand Gorge advance, developed 16,000 years ago. Ice tongues poured into the Schoharie Valley and topped the escarpment wall at Kaaterskill and Platte Cloves, further carving and eroding the northeastern Catskills. Alpine glaciation redeveloped in the southern and western Catskills enhancing the more complex local topography.

As Earth's climate warmed, the ice sheets melted faster than they advanced. Ice melted from the southern Catskills first. As the Wisconsin Ice Sheet disintegrated, ice dams hemmed large glacial lakes. Few signs of these short-lived lakes remain beyond the rock flours and delta terraces that coated lake bottoms. Large meltwater rivers widened valleys while cutting and enlarging gaps. Underfit valleys and wide steep notches resulted. Underfit valleys form when torrents of glacial meltwater widen valleys. After the ice melts, the remaining river valley is much wider than needed to hold the river. Underfit valleys in the Catskills include the Delaware and Susquehanna Rivers, and the Esopus and Schoharie Creeks. Prominent notches include Stony Clove and Mill Wheel Gap. Glacial tills—unsorted sediments carried in the ice—covered the entire region. Deepest in the valleys, the tills thin toward mountain summits. Transported boulders pepper the landscape.

Measurements estimate the northern Catskills to be .5F degrees cooler than the southern Catskills. Combined with topography, the temperature difference meant the continental ice sheets eroded the northern Catskills for a longer time period. After the Wisconsin Ice Sheet retreated and during the Grand Gorge advance, the region remained cold enough to maintain alpine glaciers. The deeply carved hollows and spur ridges distinctive to the southern Catskills reflect this alpine glaciation. Smoother, more rounded slopes characterize the northern Catskills. Rock formations and stream erosion perpetuated these differences.

Alpine glaciers scalloped many of the southern peaks. Cirques are the most common alpine feature. As ice flowed down the mountainside, it eroded the land beneath it. A cirque- scalloped mountain often resembles two arms wrapped around a body. Good examples of these formations show on Mt. Tremper, Overlook Mountain, Ashokan High Point, and Balsam Mountain. Echo Lake, between Overlook and Plattekill Mountains, is the Catskills' most developed cirque. Panther Mountain, home to the Catskills' last alpine glacier, is the mountains' largest.

Majestic hemlock trees

As the warming trend continued, the last remnants of the Grand Gorge advance melted. Unlike the southern Catskills' south-flowing rivers, the northern Catskills drain into the north-flowing Schoharie Creek. Dammed by retreating ice, the Schoharie Valley became a glacial lake. Vroman's Nose, west of Middleburgh, New York provides a great overview of this ancient lake bed. The region's fertile farmlands result from the sediments deposited in this short-lived lake. The warming climate limited alpine glacier formation, and the ice sheet continued a steady northward retreat.

Other signs of glaciation mark the Catskills. North and South Lakes, located along the eastern escarpment, are kettle lakes. They formed when ice chunks melted in poorly-drained ground. Rainwater and a man-made dam enhance and replenish these lakes. Glacial striations recorded ice sheet movement as hard rocks scratched softer bedrock. Strong striations mark many Catskill Mountains, including Overlook, North, and Peekamoose. Among the Catskills' largest glacial features was a huge ice dam that stretched between Overlook Mountain and Ashokan High Point during the Wagon Wheel advance. The resulting lake submerged the entire Esopus Valley. The lake cut Mill Wheel Gap on Ashokan High Point's southeastern flank as it drained.

Glaciation, probably related to the Illinoisian Ice Sheet's advance one million years ago, formed the Catskills' cloves. Cloves hold steep watercourses that grade into the mountain walls. The ice sheets scoured and steepened already rugged slopes. Caught between surrounding mountain peaks, these streambeds drop more than 1,000 feet per mile. Three major cloves cut into the mountains: Kaaterskill Clove, Platte Clove, and Woodland Valley. Often inaccessible, man rarely visits the streambeds nestled in the clove bottoms. Best known for their scenery and waterfalls, the cloves attract many summer visitors. Platte Clove is the Catskills' most rugged area. In its reaches are 14 waterfalls higher than 20 feet. Kaaterskill Clove is home to Kaaterskill Falls, New York's highest waterfall. Woodland Valley's steep slopes nestle against Slide Mountain.

Catskill soils directly relate to the area's past glacial activity. Most are inceptisols (young, poorly developed soils) derived from materials left by the last ice sheet, recent erosion, and biological processes. Slide Mountain's summit, which probably remained uncovered during the last continental ice sheet, has an older soil. The Catskills' mineral soil evolved from glacial till and outwash. In valleys, these soils can reach 200 feet deep, but mountaintops often have only an inch or two. Rocks are endemic in local soils as attested on the region's farms. Thousands of miles of stone fences run throughout the Catskills. Fragipans—soils bonded into a natural cement—occur frequently. Plant roots cannot penetrate fragipans, restricting growth and support.

The Catskills' rocks are an encrypted guidebook to the mountains' geology. Earthquakes, ancient seas, and possibly, meteorite impacts helped shape the Catskills. Traces of this past remain bound in local rocks.

The Acadian Mountains were a constant sediment source through-out the Devonian Period. Along with plant and animal remains, they created a continuous fossil and deposition record. Although few large fossils have been found, an excellent fossil record developed. The Catskills preserve the most complete record of Earth's Devonian history. Local rocks link events throughout the prehistoric world, serving as a template for other dating studies. The area's steady deposition of eroded material is free of faulting, folding, or bending. It is an easy record to read and understand.

Catskill fossil explorations often end in disappointment. Few good specimens are large enough to be considered noteworthy; however, near Gilboa Dam is a petrified forest. The fern-like trees grew 40 feet high. During the age of fishes, these unpopulated forests resembled modern palm forests. The western Catskills contain scattered fossil beds of marine and freshwater fish. Brachiopods, clam-like mollusks, are also common.

The Catskills' only economically valuable non-living resources are water and bluestone. Early explorers told wild stories of gold and silver, but none proved true. Along the range's southeastern edge an unusual deposit of selenite gypsum crystals formed from the retreating freshwater sea. Some people believe that oil lies beneath the mountains, and that regional water interests suppress this information.

While oil shales are common, and a potential source for future oil, no geological evidence supports claims of oil beneath the Catskills.

The Panther Mountain Circle is a puzzling and unique Catskill landform. Together, the Esopus Creek and Woodland Valley outline an almost four-mile circle. Panther Mountain's summit dominates the circle's center. Topographic studies and satellite photos raise further questions about this conspicuous feature. One hypothesis suggests that this circle outlines a meteorite crater. The region lay beneath a shallow sea when the impact occurred. Salt domes, like those found along the Mississippi Delta, are another possibility. Another hypothesis combines these ideas, proposing that after impact, the sea bed broke, crumbled, and distorted, forming a deep pool. When the sea retreated, the isolated pool evaporated and left the salt deposits.

Although a crater would form on impact, the current landscape rises into a 3,720-foot mountain. This apparent paradox could occur because salt and crushed rock are less dense than intact rock. Large amounts of lighter materials will produce a gravitational low point. With less gravity, erosional potentials are decreased. A natural, radial drainage pattern accented the process. Millions of years magnified the gravitational low point, producing an uplifted area. Panther Mountain's rugged terrain makes accurate measurements difficult. Research continues into this mystery.

The Blackhead Mountains are another geologically distinctive area. Their three summits form a high ridge in the northeastern Catskills. They rise 400 feet above surrounding peaks, and sprout no large side ridges. Rocks composing the Blackheads are older than neighboring regions. A search for earthquake faults could reveal uplift, but evidence remains circumstantial. The Blackhead's geologic history remains unknown.

THE ESCARPMENT

The escarpment wall captures the spirit of the 19th-century Catskills. Beautiful scenes unfold from atop the escarpment. Magnificent waterfalls, lofty overlooks, and deep gorges characterize the area. In addition to the high wall rising from the Hudson Valley, the area also includes Kaaterskill and Platte Cloves, Huckleberry Point, Kaaterskill High Peak and Roundtop.

Looking west from Inspiration Point—Hunter and Onteora Mountains

Hike 1: The Escarpment Wall—Pine Orchard to Sunset Rock

Roundtrip Hiking Distance: 2.6 miles

County and Town: Greene, Hunter

Parking: Take County Route 18 from Haines Falls. Enter North Lake Camping Area (access trail near picnic area).

Difficulty: easy-moderate

Bushwhack: no

Elevation Gain: (to highest point along trail, not destination) 250 feet

Going North:

Mile   0.0: Begin at Pine Orchard (site of the Catskill Mountain House), head north (blue markers)

0.5: Artist's Rock

1.1: Newman's Ledge, head east on yellow spur trail

1.3: Sunset Rock; retrace route back to Pine Orchard

2.6: Return to Pine Orchard

Hike 2: The Escarpment Wall—Schutt Road to Sunset Rock and Inspiration Point (south)

Roundtrip Hiking Distance: 2.4 miles

County and Town: Greene, Hunter

Parking: Before entrance to North/South Lake State Campground (parking area at the end of Schutt Road)

Difficulty: moderate

Bushwhack: no

Elevation Gain: 250 feet

Mile   0.0: Park at southern end of Schutt Road. Carefully cross stream.

0.0: At 3-way trail junction, follow Escarpment Trail west (blue markers)

0.7: Layman Monument; trail bends to the east

1.1: Junction with yellow-blazed trail; continue on Escarpment Trail

1.2: Sunset Rock

1.4: Inspiration Point; turn back

1.7: Junction with yellow-blazed trail; follow it north to Schutt Road Trail (red markers)

2.2: Trail ends at Schutt Road Trail; continue north (bear west)

2.4: Return to 3-way trail junction; cross stream to Schutt Road

Nothing defines the public's perception of the Catskill Mountains better than its eastern escarpment. Even today, with the Catskills best known for wilderness and recreation, memories of grand hotels remain associated with its lofty eastern escarpment. The Catskill Mountain House was richest in fame and history. Its thirteen Corinthian columns overlooked 50 miles of the Hudson River for more than a century. Although the Mountain House is gone, the surrounding area still delights the eye and spirit.

South Mountain, North Mountain, Roundtop, and Kaaterskill High Peak made popular hiking destinations. Kaaterskill High Peak, promoted as the mighty Catskills' highest peak, became the western hemisphere's most visited mountaintop. Local hotel owners continued to maintain its height superiority long after geographers measured higher Catskill summits. Today, Kaaterskill High Peak stands in relative obscurity; few people know about the mountain's storied past. Gentler paths followed North and South Lakes. The lakes feed Lake Creek, marking one of Kaaterskill Clove's heads. A trail follows the clove to the 260-foot, two-tiered Kaaterskill Falls. Vacationers also hiked escarpment trails to Artist's Rock, Newman's Ledge, Sunrise Rock, and Sunset Rock.

Distinctive mountain vistas, coupled with history, ecology, and discovery, produce one of eastern North America's most attractive places. Generations of wealthy Americans vacationed here, making it the New World's premier summer resort. While high society no longer cools in the summer breezes, people come in record numbers to enjoy the local beauty.

The Catskills' escarpment wall rises seven miles west of the Hudson River. Its hard sandstone and soft shale cliffs rise 2,000 feet in a half mile. The eastern escarpment stretches 30 miles, from Overlook Mountain north to Windham High Peak. A series of parallel, horizontal rock layers and ridges characterize the escarpment. They provide some of the Catskills' most enchanting vistas. The most famous surround North and South Lakes and the Pine Orchard.

More than any other local landmark, the Catskill Mountain House symbolizes the Catskill Mountains. Opened in 1823 by the Beach family, it attracted high society to the Catskills. They came for the cool summer air and the mountain vistas. The ride to the Mountain House was at first a twisting, grueling carriage ride from Catskill. In the 1880s, the Otis Elevating Railroad delivered guests in relative comfort. A treeless scar marks the railroad's climb. It tops the escarpment below the Pine Orchard. Hotel Kaaterskill, a larger, fancier hotel located a half mile south of Pine Orchard, rivaled the Catskill Mountain House in luxury, but never in status.

The Catskill Mountain House remained in operation until 1942. Abandoned and neglected, the structure decayed. In 1963, New

York State burned the hotel's carcass to protect visitors from injury. This historic spot, the keystone of society's 19th-century recreation in the Catskills, remains only in memory, imagery, and words.

Thomas Cole, founder of the Hudson River School of Landscape Painting, sketched out many of his greatest works from the escarpment. Cole's *View of Two Lakes and the Mountain House, Catskill Mountains,* and *Sunrise in the Catskill Mountains*, depict the 19th-century scenery. The Hudson River School's paintings helped promote the Catskills' growing reputation as a summer resort.

The attention given the escarpment centered upon its extraordinary location and scenery. Its natural beauty resulted from the forces that shaped the landscape. The Catskills' escarpment wall matured when continental ice sheets flowed down the Hudson Valley. Contained by the escarpment, the ice sheets scoured the shale and sandstone wall. Once the ice sheets topped the Catskills' eastern front, they rounded slopes and produced new drainage patterns. In places, after the ice sheets retreated, chunks of ice remained embedded in newly exposed lands. Impermeable rocks trapped the melting ice waters. Kettle lakes, including North and South Lakes, resulted.

When the ice sheets melted, they deposited unsorted sediments atop the Catskills. These tills provided the mineral component to local soils. Only a small amount of material covered the escarpment, resulting in its thin, infertile soils. Spent needles, leaves, and plants provide the soil's organic component. The thin soils, jointed bedrock, and strong sunlight create dry conditions. Fires can occur in dry years. Fire-adapted plants such as pitch pine, chestnut oak, mountain laurel, blueberries, and galax do well in this environment, and are common. Cooler, moister conditions encouraged northern hardwoods forests to grow a few miles to the west.

A dam has increased the size and recreational potential of North and South Lakes. It also changed the lakes' character, combining the two into a single body. Although artificially altered, the lakes retain their romantic setting and beautiful vistas while offering a cool summer retreat. A State-run campground surrounds the lakeshore.

From the Catskill Mountain House's front porch, guests looked out upon sloops and other sailing ships trafficking the Hudson. Although the escarpment's great hotels faded into history, the area's natural beauty and grace remain. The emerald green and subtle blues of the Hudson Valley stretch to the east, lifting into Connecticut, Massachusetts, and Vermont's highest points. Clear mountain waters lap on the lakeshore, while Kaaterskill High Peak and Roundtop loom in the distance.

The escarpment trail wraps along the Catskills' steep eastern edge, unveiling a series of extraordinary views. Sunset Rock, located along the northern wall of Kaaterskill Clove, provides one of the best vistas in the Catskill Mountains. The escarpment trail outlines South Mountain above Kaaterskill Falls before curving east to parallel Kaaterskill Clove. Wet and dry sites, enhanced by drainage, exposure, and topography combine forest elements of the Hudson Valley with the those of the Catskills. The forest is a mix of hickory, oak, pine, maple, birch, and beech. Mountain laurel, host to a prolific show of pink and white flowers in mid-June, and striped maple dominate much of the understory. Then, without introduction, the forest parts and the trail opens onto a smooth rock floor.

Sunset Rock is a wide, flat ledge. To the east is the Hudson Valley, directly south stand Kaaterskill High Peak and Roundtop, and to the west is Hunter Mountain. One giant step below the ledge is Kaaterskill Clove. Onteora Mountain rises above the clove, its presence more distinct from this view than elsewhere in the Catskills. The youthful stream's raw power echos off the clove walls, filling the scene with a muted roar. Haines Falls, Kaaterskill Creek's most impressive drop, tumbles down the clove's southwestern face. Smaller waterfalls scattered throughout the clove glow a frothy white against the red, green, and brown backdrop. Stream erosion cuts small V-shaped valleys into the U-shaped clove. Landslides pock the mountainsides, leaving scars second in prominence only to man's structures clinging to the tenacious slopes.

Trails atop the escarpment wall provided access to the inspiring scenes painted by Thomas Cole more than a century and a half ago. Artist's Rock, Prospect Point, Lookout Rock, Inspiration Point, Profile Rock, and other vistas line the Catskills' eastern front. A thick spruce-fir forest grows atop the nearby peaks to create a black line against the crisp blue sky. Overall, the mountains remain as they did a century ago; however, man's impressions of them are different. Preservation and discovery replaced exploitation and dominance. Local trails provide a route to reflect on these changes and trace the steps that helped them occur.

Unfortunately, not all the changes are good. The natural features suffer from heavy recreational use. Litter abounds in the grasses and forest. Crowded hiking trails can resemble a city street. Silence disappears as hundreds of people chatter about the area's beauty. Soils erode and compact, tree roots break and die, and waste needs processing and removal. A chain-link fence protects people from falling down the mountainside. Or is it there to keep humans out? These features betoken a land under siege. People are loving it to death.

More than any other place in the Catskills, the escarpment near North and South Lakes requires careful, active stewardship. Its attractions and links with the past, supported by history and art, remain compelling. Crowded conditions and conquered wilderness provide a benchmark for comparison with the untamed backcountry.

Despite changes in the land and its use, the escarpment remains a majestic site. Perhaps it is the glorious, colorful sunrises over the Hudson River. Maybe it is something abstract, manufactured in people's hearts, rather than a product of the land. Whatever the case, the escarpment, Pine Orchard, and North and South Lakes are special places. The same qualities that made it an icon in the past will endear it to future generations.

HUCKLEBERRY POINT

Hike: Huckleberry Point
Roundtrip Hiking Distance: 4.6 miles
County and Town: Greene, Hunter
Parking: Off Platte Clove Road, near the head of the clove (on south side of road, just west of stone bridge).
Difficulty: easy-moderate
Bushwhack: no
Elevation Gain: (to highest point along trail, not destination) 650 feet
Mile 0.0: State marked snowmobile trail begins at the top of Platte Clove
1.1: Side trail heads east (right) for Huckleberry Point
1.5: Cross Plattekill Creek
1.9: Crest a small rise; begin descent
2.3: Reach Huckleberry Point, go back via same route
4.6: Return to trailhead.

Not every destination in the Catskills sits atop the mountains, and not every inspiring view lies where the mountains meet the sky. The Catskills' flanks and ridges sprout ledges and cliffs that also survey the surrounding lands. Special places sit between soaring mountaintops and rushing waters, combining and accenting the experience of both. Huckleberry Point is such a place.

Located on Kaaterskill High Peak's southeastern corner, Huckleberry Point's inspiring ledges overlook the placid Hudson Valley and rugged Platte Clove. Perched at the junction of valley, clove, and mountain wall, Huckleberry Point stands between manicured fields and wilderness. As an easy two-mile hike, when time is short, its rewarding views and majestic setting are the equal of many longer treks.

The trail to Huckleberry Point begins where Platte Clove Road tops its namesake. The abandoned dirt road, now a hiking and snow-

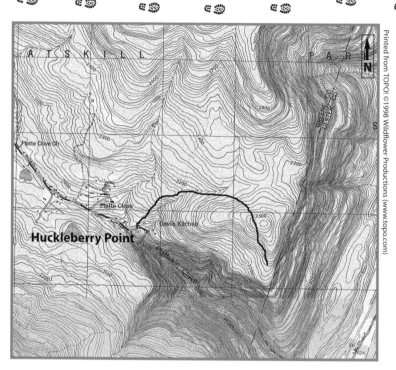

mobile trail, heads toward Kaaterskill High Peak and Roundtop. Logged early in the 20th century, the recovering land supports a vigorous second growth forest. The road slowly lifts through a forest of hemlock, yellow birch, paper birch, northern red oak, and beech. An occasional red spruce, unusual at 2,000 feet, mixes with the forest in cool and shady niches.

The dirt road, once a town road, is an eroded mess. Sunken up to two feet in places, the rocky, muddy course resulted from massive erosion. This minor environmental disaster is a direct result of poor road construction. The road was once a maintained town road, but more recently it, along with many new side roads, was used for logging. Logging companies built their roads so they could quickly and cheaply extract the region's timber. Constructed without water bars, culverts, or switchbacks, the overused roads became lanes of compacted soil. Vegetation cannot grow in the cemented dirt, and water cannot penetrate its surface. The result is that water flows along the road, gaining energy and removing soil and rock. Over time this process produced the depressed, puddle-saturated roadbed.

The recessed road climbs slowly through the forest, its poor condition a constant feature. After a few twists, a side trail heads east to Huckleberry Point. The trail is marked by small white disks with a red spot, but following the trail can become confusing. Poorly spaced markers and the thin track often mislead. Still, this unobtrusive trail is a pleasant change from the more heavily used roads and paths crisscrossing this forest. In the late fall and winter, the trail often fades into the leaf or snow covered landscape. To the northwest rise Kaaterskill High Peak and Roundtop, 1,400 feet higher than this shelf.

Birch and hemlock dominate the forest, complemented by northern red oak, beech, red spruce, and black cherry. Striped maple, beech saplings, ferns, and mosses grow beneath the canopy. Mountain laurel mix into the understory as the path progresses. At first, the laurel's presence is sporadic, but then builds into large stands of entangling limbs. Tangles of waxy leaves and sinewy branches grow eight feet high. Soon, the laurel clusters become so dense that the trail provides the only passable route. In spring, the laurel's pink and white flowers make a spectacular display.

After cresting a small ridge, the trail begins a gentle descent. The environment becomes drier. Dense stands of mountain laurel monopolize the understory. Forest composition changes. A thick, crisp leaf litter blankets the forest floor. Each step kicks up a storm of brittle sound. Tall white pines rise into and beyond the forest canopy, but northern red oak dominates the landscape. Paper birch's stark white trunks gleam in the sunlight in contrast with rich blue skies.

Northern hardwoods dominate most of the Catskills, but as the trail to Huckleberry Point progresses, it moves into a pine-oak forest. The well-drained, sun-drenched slopes create dry habitats and higher soil temperatures. Other environmental changes, especially related to nutrient cycling, accompany this transition. The thick layer of leaf litter develops as the resident oak leaves, full of tannin, decay slower than most other species. Dead leaves and needles become the major storehouse for nutrients, preventing the higher temperatures from releasing them too quickly. The tannins, indigestible by most animals and insects, also deter consumption.

The trail descends a series of ridges and shelves as it heads east. A ridgeline blocks the northern view, while glimpses south reveal Plattekill and Indian Head Mountains. A few sugar maples join the foliage, as the moister soils can support a more diverse stand. Paper birch trunks paint white lines through the forest. Other species joining the community are yellow birch, black cherry, pitch pine, chestnut oak, and beech.

As the trail weaves along increasingly rocky terrain, the ridgetop forest thins. Poor soils exclude many of the northern hardwoods. Large rock outcrops, many covered with lichens such as rock tripe, pepper the ground. Pitch pine becomes the dominant tree, developing into thick stands of small, twisted evergreens. A few chestnut oak round out this dry pine-oak forest, dominant for the journey's duration.

The pitch pine groves and surrounding areas are virgin forest. This area escaped logging; the trees are economically worthless. Yellowgreen needles create a lush appearance throughout the year. The mature grove resembles the Catskill Mountain House site, Pine Orchard, before its development in the 1820s. The dry, exposed, windswept environment shortens tree stature and lifespan, but keeps the area relatively warm. On sunny days, Huckleberry Point is often 15F degrees warmer than surrounding areas.

Forests along the Catskills' eastern escarpment are dry, hostile environments. This is not due to a lack of precipitation—the area receives more than 50 inches per year—but because of thin soils and steep slopes. They drain quickly, allowing the forest floor to dry. Pitch pine need fire to regenerate. Without this heat to release their seeds, saplings cannot sprout. The large number of current pitch pines attests to past fires. The area's light and moderate burns consume excess fuel and release nutrients for the next generation of growth. Fire suppres-

A southwest view from Huckleberry Point—Indian Head, Twin, and Spruce Top Mountains

sion, man's dominant policy over the past century, limited pitch pine regeneration, but fire is an essential part of this environment. The area's other major species—galax, huckleberries, mountain laurel, and chestnut oak—all do best in dry, fire-prone habitats.

Huckleberry Point opens as the dense pitch pines yield to rocky slopes. Trees survive only in scattered pockets, their twisted and battered limbs a reflection of the harsh environment. True to its name, huckleberries cover the landscape. In summer they provide a tasty snack, attracting wildlife and humans.

Cliff faces herald steep drops to the south and east, clearing the skyline of vegetation for a 180-degree panorama. Rock ledges provide an intense and unique view of the Catskills and surrounding lowlands. Across Platte Clove's dark, wild depths is Plattekill Mountain. The lands between the 3,100-foot mountaintop and the Clove's bottom

2,000 feet below are among the roughest terrain in the eastern United States. In the clove, the stream continues its work, sculpting ever deeper into the land. Its constant roar washes up to Huckleberry Point.

Beyond Plattekill Mountain, Overlook Mountain juts into the Hudson Valley, its metal towers slicing the sky. The soft, wide valley escorts the tidal river as it parallels the Catskills' escarpment. To the southeast, the Kingston-Rhinecliff bridge spans the mile-wide river. As the land moves west from the river, it rises as the Hudson Valley builds into the Catskills' eastern front. Mount Marion marks the first major climb, followed by a low plateau that blends into the Catskills' higher reaches.

The Taconics—once a great mountain chain, now a low range of hills—rise east of the Hudson Valley. Kingston, first capital of New York, nestles along the river. Another low mountain range, the Shawangunks, leads southwest from Kingston. The Ashokan Reservoir sits between this sharp range and Overlook Mountain. The Devil's Path Mountains loom in the southwest: Indian Head, Twin, Sugarloaf, and Spruce Top.

Indian Head rises to 3,573 feet above sea level, looming above Platte Clove and Huckleberry Point. Perched between the aspiring peaks and deep valleys, Huckleberry Point provides an excellent perspective of Catskill elevations. From the Hudson's tidal banks to Indian Head's summit, 3,573 feet of elevation are visible.

Kaaterskill High Peak's mass builds northwest from Huckleberry Point. A series of animal trails lead through boulder fields and dense laurel stands to higher lookouts. About 200 feet above the open vistas, a resistant sandstone layer overlooks Huckleberry Point and its environs. The challenging climb through unmarked forest and rock walls is an adventure. The unblazed lands continue to rise, offering additional perspectives of the landscape.

The junction of the warmer, flatter Hudson Valley with the cooler mountains produces an atmosphere rich in turbulence. Rising thermals provide excellent habitats for raptors. Turkey vultures and red-tailed hawks commonly soar among the rising heat waves. As their keen eyes search for prey or carrion, the winds help glide the circling aviators.

The swirling currents often bring these magnificent birds near Huckleberry Point, a great place to observe these graceful creatures.

Huckleberry Point is a refreshing, inspiring site, offering the senses a special show. Mountains, trees, valleys, and streams create a wild and rugged scene, yet it is secure and placid. A trip to these rocky perches often removes a chill from the air and calms the spirit. It is a short, easy hike, well worth the effort.

At Huckleberry Point looking east at the Hudson Valley

PLATTE CLOVE

Hike: Platte Clove
One-way Hiking Distance: 2.0 miles
County and Town: Ulster, Saugerties
Difficulty: very difficult,
    not a recommended hike
Bushwhack: yes, route generally
    follows streambed
Elevation Gain: 1300 feet

Not a recommended hike

Only two breaches penetrate the mountain barrier of the Catskills' eastern escarpment, cutting it into crumbled slices of fortress wall. Streams, ice, and time worked to carve these rugged insets. Grain by grain, and at times, boulder by boulder, water degraded the escarpment. Kaaterskill Clove is the larger breach. To its south, Platte Clove is a smaller, more rugged wilderness. Home to Plattekill Creek, this untamed landscape is among the Appalachians' most difficult terrain.

Platte and Kaaterskill Cloves are young. They were born during the era of the Illinoisan Ice Sheet. After this continental glacier retreated a million years ago, the action of wind, water, and ice expanded the cloves. Erosional processes, however, are not uniform. Subsequent ice sheets reworked the deepening stream valleys, adding glacial landforms to the sheer walls. The most recent water erosion carved V-shaped valley floors below the cloves' U-shaped walls.

Platte Clove's topography is sharp and steep. Plattekill Creek's streambed climbs from 700 to 2,200 feet in less than two miles. Natural features split the clove in two. The lower section is a canyon nestled between Plattekill Mountain and Kaaterskill High Peak's shadows. The clear waters cascade through oversized beds of smooth boulders and

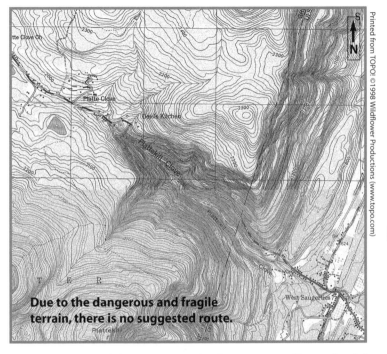

Printed from TOPO! ©1998 Wildflower Productions (www.topo.com)

Due to the dangerous and fragile terrain, there is no suggested route.

gravel. Deprived of the sun's warmth, the water is cold. Much of the flow is beneath the surface, percolating though the streambed's thick lining. A series of small waterfalls, up to 25 feet, and deep plunge pools separate quieter stretches with jumps and bounces. Each fall gushes jets of water from resistant sandstone ledges, carving smooth tracks into the thick, gray rocks. Many resemble natural waterslides. Crystal green-blue tinted pools, actually more than 15 feet deep, appear to hold only a few inches of water. Multi-colored stones, dominated by red, green, gray and beige, line the stream bottom.

Platte Clove's vegetation is a unique mix of northern hardwoods. In the lower clove, hemlock and yellow birch grow along the cool, damp streambanks. White ash, American basswood, and sugar maple live on the clove's floor. Northern red oak and white pine grow a short distance upslope, away from the stream's influence. Beech, intolerant of saturated soils, live throughout the clove except along the stream. More than 100 wildflower species flourish in the sunny glades; lesser numbers bloom in the shaded forest.

Platte Clove's upper half is much different than the lower canyon. The landscape is steeper and more rugged. Cliffs abound, and 70-foot waterfalls leap their heights, sending the stream vertical. Sharp rocks and angled boulders fill and define the stream's course, while gravels and sands quickly wash downstream among torrents of east-flowing water. Only a few isolated pockets hold these smaller materials. The graceful, placid pools common along the stream's lower half are absent. Their formation is not even a possibility in the water's rush to lose potential energy to gravity.

The clove's walls remain steep, but their towering heights drop as the streambed gains elevation. Small rockslides mar the clove's craggy walls, memorials to a war between stability and gravity. The land trades Hudson Valley softness for Catskill Mountain character. Direct sunlight returns to the clove bottom, warming the water, land, and air. The hemlock's deep, cool shade disappears on the exposed slopes. The sunny, warm surfaces provide prime snake habitat. Rattlesnakes and copperheads occasionally bask on the sun-painted outcrops.

Waterfalls are common throughout the clove. In geologic terms, Plattekill Creek is a young, active stream, with waterfalls, cascades, and high erosion rates. Water rushes down the steep valleys so quickly that floodplain development is minimal. Over millions of years, these youthful streams erode their courses into smooth, wide plains. Before that occurs here, future ice sheets will probably alter this landscape beyond recognition. In the short term, Plattekill Creek will continue to expand the clove's western limits. Eventually, it may capture some of the Schoharie Creek's headwaters, altering the area's basic drainage. An act of stream piracy, this event would greatly enlarge Plattekill Creek's volume and further increase erosion rates.

Two varieties of sedimentary rocks dominate Platte Clove. Oneonta sandstones and red shales form the clove's lower half. Harder Hamilton sandstones, gray in color, dominate the higher areas. Often

Plattekill Clove Falls

the series mix, layering thin red rocks with thicker gray sandstones. The colorful interface results from environmental conditions 360 million years ago. Rock color often reveals deposition conditions. Red rocks contain oxidized iron (rust), while green rocks have reduced iron. Gray rocks have reduced iron, or are iron poor. Red rocks denote a land or shallow water deposition, while reduced iron reveals a deep water burial.

The Oneonta formation erodes faster than the Hamilton. Overhangs and ledges of gray sandstone result. Waterfalls form when water reaches these overhangs. In Platte Clove's upper half, the dominant sandstones produce smaller overhangs, but support higher cliffs.

Despite its isolation, Platte Clove shows signs of heavy impact and abuse. A well-worn trail parallels the stream's lower half. Short, easy hikes access the lower pools and waterfalls. Here, in a place so wild that man's technologies remain unknown, humankind scorns mother nature with litter, overused and illegal campsites, and erosional disasters. Such unwelcome sites are common in the clove—the gift of an ungrateful public.

Undrinkable water is one result of man's mistreatment. *Giardia*, a small disease-causing organism, lives in most Catskill streams. Introduced from animal waste, mainly dogs and horses, the cysts, if ingested, can cause severe intestinal tract distress. Dehydration and weight loss are common symptoms. Despite its clear, pure appearance, all Catskill Mountain water requires treatment. Boiling, filtration, or chemicals will kill *Giardia*.

It is easy to reach the lower pools and waterfalls, but paths to the upper clove are obscure and dangerous. The trail ends at the boundary separating the lower and upper clove. A waterfall marks the border. One last pool collects at the fall's base. The fall is a hybrid of the clove's two varieties. Above this point the clove's walls approach vertical. Except where waterfalls preclude its use, the streambed is the only trail.

The streambed splits as it climbs higher into the escarpment. Near the clove's upper terminus, the streambed degrades into a collection of huge, angular boulders. The route consists of scaling from one large, rough-hewn rock to another. Each step brings the mountain masses closer. Views into the Hudson Valley, framed by Huckleberry Point and Plattekill Mountain, open as the clove's floor gains elevation. Rock ledges supporting the waterfalls provide the best platforms. A set of high, steep cliffs quickly bring the streambed closer to the surrounding terrain. After reaching Plattekill Falls, part of a reserve owned by the Catskill Center for Conservation and Development, the journey ends. A nature trail leads back to Platte Clove Road. Plattekill Creek continues into the mountains as a set of feeder streams.

🚶🚶

The best way to explore Platte Clove is to climb the streambed. It is a challenging and difficult adventure. Only the most experienced and hearty hikers should attempt this trek. Not only is it dangerous—the land itself cannot handle the damage caused by humans as they scurry up the almost impassible landscape. While not a recommended hike, Platte Clove's character is such an important piece of the Catskills' mosaic that a description of the route is necessary to fully appreciate some the Catskills' most amazing spots.

Along the clove's lower half, the large pools filling the valley make it impossible to remain along the stream and stay dry. The heavy shade keeps water temperatures below 60F degrees. The path follows a ledge above the streambed, bypassing its pools and waterfalls. Most places along the stream make for great rock hopping, but an occasional swim is necessary.

Waterfalls often require climbing nearby rock faces. The pools and waterfalls continue until the valley bottom changes from water carved (V-shaped) to ice carved (U-shaped).

After this point, the trip becomes more challenging and dangerous. The clove's walls are steeper, and the falls are higher. Rainbow Falls, a 70-foot plunge, requires a detour along the clove's southern wall. Accompanied by rapids, the stream falls more than 120 feet in this turbulent corridor. A steep, narrow path circles the fall. Loose rocks and soils make a shower of debris as they slip down the sheer slopes. Careful foot placement becomes first priority.

Above Rainbow Falls, the streambed degrades into a series of sharp boulders. Within these rocky depths the clove splits; the small waterfall near the fork holds the overlook into the Hudson Valley. Above the junction, a high spur protrudes from the Catskills' mountain wall and separates the stream's two branches. The northern branch retains Plattekill Creek, but traverses private land. The southern branch provides a more accessible route. Still, the valley is little more than a rockslide squeezed between precipitous walls. During normal flow, the water rushes below the boulders. Although the slopes are steep, progress is rapid. Plattekill Falls, is more than 1,500 feet above the clove's bottom.

Platte Clove is among the northeastern United States' most inaccessible regions. Its spectacular waterfalls provide some of the Catskills' wildest scenery. In contrast, the beautiful crystal pools that fill the clove's lower canyon are among the area's most peaceful spots. Lush flora thrive in the humid conditions wherever soil accumulates. Platte Clove's forest communities cover the range of vegetation found from the Hudson Valley to the Catskills' upper elevations. Together, these features make the clove a unique and spectacular place.

KAATERSKILL HIGH PEAK

Hike: Kaaterskill High Peak
Circuit Hiking Distance: 6.6 miles
County and Town: Greene, Hunter
Parking: Off Platte Clove Road, (on south side of road, just west of stone bridge). Trail is on north side of road
Difficulty: difficult
Bushwhack: yes (about 1.5 miles), but optional
Elevation Gain: 1650 feet
Mile 0.0: State-marked snowmobile trail begins at the top of Platte Clove
  3.5: Long Path separates and heads for Palenville; remain on snowmobile trail
  3.7: Turn south on trail marked with blue paint
  4.4: Summit of Kaaterskill High Peak
  4.7: Hurricane Ridge
  5.1: Junction with snowmobile trail on south side of mountain, begin bushwhack (145-degree bearing)
  6.2: Bushwhack ends; return to original trail
  6.6: Return to trailhead.

Kaaterskill High Peak, the Catskills' 21st highest peak, rises to 3,655 feet. In the 19th century, during the era of the Catskill Mountain House, many proclaimed this prominent peak the Catskills' highest. Despite evidence disputing the falsehood, local resort owners boasted of grandiose hotels built in the tallest peak's shadow. Accurate measurements were not accepted until the late 1870s. Even then, hotel owners and local leaders defended Kaaterskill High Peak's premier elevational status.

No longer do the great hotels draw people to the eastern Catskills, leaving Kaaterskill High Peak as an obscure mountain lining the Hudson Valley. Despite heavy visitation in the 1800s, no major trail leads to its summit. The current path traverses steep slopes and swampy ground as it winds up the mountainside. Some areas are wet most of the year, dampening even hearty spirits. A bushwhack is often drier and more pleasurable than the mucky, established route.

Kaaterskill High Peak and its 3,440-foot companion, Roundtop, stand out along the Catskills' skyline. The two peaks sail through the sky, their eastern slopes eternally poised over the eastern escarpment and Hudson Valley. Roundtop trails Kaaterskill High Peak like a child not wishing to lose his mother. Together, the mountains are a perfect combination of strength, grace, and family, as though a master plan ensured they form on this site.

Kaaterskill High Peak and the surrounding area has a rich history. During the Revolutionary War, the British and their Iroquois allies used the mountain to spy on rebelling colonists. In the mid and late 1800s, the summit was a popular tourist destination. On hot summer days, hikers flocked to Kaaterskill High Peak's cool slopes. Most believed they hiked to the Catskills' highest summit; many of them died without ever knowing the truth. After the area's tourism declined in the early 1900s, visitation to Kaaterskill High Peak slowed. Today, only the occasional outdoorsman experiences its slopes and vistas.

Of the marked trails leading toward Kaaterskill High Peak's summit, the shortest route begins at Platte Clove's western head. The path follows an old logging road. Glacial till, up to a foot thick, lines the roadbed's deep sidecuts. Till is the glacially deposited silt, sand, and rock beneath the thin organic soil. The trail—part abandoned town road, part castaway logging road—moves through a different world than in the area's more developed past. Poor construction techniques and subsequent erosion resulted in today's sunken roadbed. The trail, a collection of ruts and rills, will remain in disrepair as the land decays around this open wound. The roadbed becomes less of a scar and more trail-like as it heads through the young, vibrant forest. Small streams and scenic openings highlight the path. The winding trail is not steep. Water, not slope, is the main obstacle. Skill and luck must combine favorably in order to remain dry.

Kaaterskill High Peak's lower forests are second growth. Only the spruce-fir and upper hardwood forests covering its top 350 feet are vir-

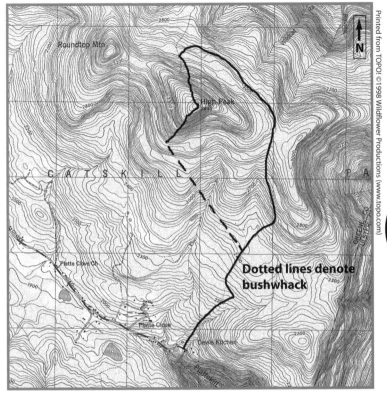

gin forest. In the upper elevations, dark green, aromatic conifers mix with paper birch, yellow birch, mountain-ash, black cherry, and fire cherry. A few large trees sprawl among the hordes of small stems that characterize this wind-battered forest. Below these virgin tracts, young northern hardwoods dominate the landscape. Sugar maple, red maple, beech, and black cherry are common. Patches of northern red oak inhabit dry, rocky ledges. Hemlocks line the streams, outgrowing other species in these cooler, damper microenvironments. Mountain laurel, hobblebush, and sugar maple and beech saplings compose the sparse understory. Ferns and flowers thrive in the sunny gaps.

Above the heavily-logged areas easily accessed from the Schoharie Valley, Kaaterskill High Peak's middle slopes reveal an older northern hardwood forest—mainly sugar maple and beech, along with yellow birch, striped maple, red maple, and black cherry. Hemlocks remain entrenched along the stream courses. Red spruce also add an occasional swath of stiff evergreen to the deciduous woods.

The marked route includes a short section of State-maintained snowmobile loop. Situated on a 3,100-foot ledge, this route encircles Kaaterskill High Peak and Roundtop, but does not approach either summit. The red, gray, and green sandstones have many snowmobile scars. To the untrained eye the scratches can appear natural. A glacial striation occurs when a hard rock embedded in an ice sheet scours the underlying bedrock. These directional marks are common in the Catskills. At this site, however, close inspection reveals fresh cuts in all directions, not the parallel grooves of glacial striations.

The wet snowmobile trail loops around Kaaterskill High Peak's eastern face to a trail marked with blue paint. This unofficial path follows the mountain's northern face to the summit. A mossy streambed shares the route's lower half. Aside from the natural sites, a small plane wreck peppers the trailside. Deformed aluminum and titanium attest to the mountain's power.

Few vistas open along this route, but a ledge near the summit reveals a partial northern view. From this vantage, Kaaterskill Clove and Kaaterskill Creek spill into the Hudson Valley. North of the clove are South Mountain's low slopes. Kaaterskill Falls' waters plummet behind the rounded slopes. The roar of the clove's active waters lift from the depths. North and South Lakes placidly sit atop the escarpment wall, while Stoppel Point and North Mountain rise west of the escarpment. Behind North Mountain, the worn, glaciated features of the East Jewett Range, Parker Hill, and Onteora Mountains parallel the Schoharie Valley. Behind them looms the Blackhead Range, rising 500 feet above this lofty overlook.

Thick evergreens monopolize Kaaterskill High Peak's summit. The thick cover of young red spruce is an impressive and impenetrable site. In the 1960s, a major red spruce decline marred the Appalachian's

Looking south from Hurricane Ridge—Plattekill, Overlook, and Indian Head Mountains

spruce-fir forests. Today, their recovery blankets many Catskill summits with crowded stands of young conifers.

The trail continues beyond the summit, heading southwest to Hurricane Ridge. Known for its high winds and heavy damage from a 1950 hurricane, this ledge offers spectacular views. The surrounding Catskills, exposed in a south-facing semicircle, are a vista worth seeing in any season. No tall trees hinder the view. Only shrub-sized fire cherry and yellow birch grow along the ridge. A high cliff prevents the trees below from eclipsing the view.

In the foreground, across the Schoharie's U-shaped valley, rise the Devil's Path Mountains. The entire ridge is in full view: Indian Head, Twin, Sugarloaf, Plateau, and Hunter Mountains. Spruce Top protrudes from Sugarloaf Mountain. East of this mighty ridgeline is Plattekill Mountain, its eastern slopes merging into the Hudson Valley. Overlook Mountain sits behind Plattekill, their slopes joined along the eastern escarpment. Slide Mountain, the highest Catskill peak, rises in the southwest, but from this distance and perspective it is hard to identify it as king among the Catskills. East of Slide are the other peaks composing the Burroughs Range: Wittenberg, Cornell, Friday, and Balsam Cap Mountains.

Beyond Hurricane Ridge, the trail quickly declines along the craggy southern face into a northern hardwood forest. After a half mile, the steep trail crosses the snowmobile trail. The warmer, drier southern slopes favor beech, striped maple, black cherry, and northern red oak. Since oak rarely grow above 3,200 feet in the Catskills, their presence here at 3,420 feet attests to this area's favorable habitat. On sunny days, temperatures at Hurricane Ridge are often 5-15F degrees warmer than at the summit. Unlike Kaaterskill High Peak's northern face, where red spruce and balsam fir grade into the forest, the cliff face here abruptly ends their presence.

When equipped with map and compass, this junction is a good place to begin a bushwhack, especially in spring and fall when leaves do not limit visibility. The State-marked trail leading to the parking area is easy to find after traversing Kaaterskill High Peak's middle elevations. From the junction with snowmobile trail, follow a southeast bearing for a mile and a quarter. The off-trail hike saves distance, time, and lots of wet ground. To move through the forest without a predefined path also bestows a degree of freedom lost when following marked trails. Even if the bearing is off, the route will still intersect the trail or Platte Clove Road. After rejoining the trail, it is a simple walk back to the trailhead.

Kaaterskill High Peak's mountain island offers many opportunities for observing nature. Forests typical of the Catskills thrive along the route. Trout lilies' yellow flowers with green and brown mottled leaves abound in early spring. About a week later, millions of spring beauties emerge. The small, purple and white, five-petaled flowers decorate the mountainside. Downy yellow, Canada, white sweet, and common violets soon bloom.

Kaaterskill High Peak and Roundtop's isolation allows animals to prosper. The undisturbed and hard-to-access habitats make the area a quality refuge. Common birds include pileated woodpeckers, chickadees, nuthatches, wild turkey, ruffed grouse, and turkey vultures. Porcupines roam the woods along with opossums, raccoons, and foxes. Small mammals ranging from the ever-present chipmunk to the gray squirrel thrive in the unspoiled mountain habitats. Larger mammals include the nimble white-tailed deer and elusive black bear.

About 450 black bears live in the Catskills. These magnificent animals are the largest creature currently roaming the region. Lower at the shoulder than the hind leg, the black bear is less intimidating and aggressive than its western cousins. Males average 350 pounds, and females 250 pounds. Only the strongest, fittest males get to mate. Cubs are born in January while mother is in a deep sleep, and they remain with her for about 18 months. In the wild, bears reach 12-15 years of age. Most die from rotted teeth. Bears that regularly eat human food and garbage rarely live more than eight years. Plastic wrappers, aluminum and metal packaging, and high salt content are serious threats to bear health.

Since wild bears have a natural fear of humans, they will run away at the first sign of people. Black bears are dangerous only if separated from their young or tempted by human food. The latter, a learned behavior, is a major reason why feeding bears is a bad idea. Fed bears quickly become dead bears. Most are hit by cars. Others are poached, or become aggressive toward people and face destruction.

Bears don't truly hibernate; they wake during mild stretches of winter weather to search for food. By late May, all the bears are awake for the season and looking for food. Their diet consists mostly of leaves, nuts, and berries. They are expert tree climbers. Insects, such as grubs, termites, and bees provide most of their protein. Fish and carrion are other sources. On rare occasions, a bear may prey upon a fawn or sick deer. Black bear attacks on humans almost always result from the bear's attraction to the food people carry.

Bears are territorial. A mother and her cubs will range over a few square miles, while a young, unestablished male may roam a few hundred square miles. Territories often overlap. As local populations expand, the juveniles must search elsewhere for suitable habitats. This often brings them in contact with people. As civilization expands, conflicts between bears and humans increase. Kaaterskill High Peak's lower slopes are one of the best bear habitats in the Catskills.

A one-time destination of the new world's social elite, Kaaterskill High Peak is now a destination almost forgotten. It is a unique natural area, even among its neighbors. It has awesome vistas, plentiful wildlife, and offers quiet relaxation. Although often overlooked by recent history, Kaaterskill High Peak is a mountain worth a day's exploration.

KAATERSKILL CLOVE

Hike: Kaaterskill Clove
One-way Hiking Distance: 2.7 miles
County and Town: Greene, Hunter
Parking: Off Route 23A, about .6 miles west of Palenville (by Fawn's Leap—pull-off on south side of road)
Difficulty: difficult
Bushwhack: yes (except for last .5 miles), route follows stream
Elevation Gain: 1200 feet
(Requires 2 vehicles)
Mile 0.0: Pick up stream 1.3 miles west of Palenville just before NY Route 23A crosses to the north bank
0.6: Pass small waterfall as it enters the clove
1.7: Kaaterskill Creek splits; head north (right) along Lake Creek
2.2: Stream rejoins road at Bastion Falls
2.7: Kaaterskill Falls; end of trip (note: State-marked trail ends .1 miles before the falls)

The village of Palenville dates to the region's Dutch colonization. Located at the Hudson Valley's western edge, the important trading town provided a gateway into the Catskills. Kaaterskill Clove begins west of Palenville as Kaaterskill Creek migrates out of the mountains. The clove's rugged terrain lifts 2,000 feet in four miles, and harbors wilderness unparalleled in the eastern United States. Spectacular mountain and white-water scenery paint the area with bold greens, blues, tans, reds, and white.

Kaaterskill Creek helped carve this wild valley. Splashing, thrusting, and eroding its way down the clove, the stream's waters tremble with energy. Although glaciers carved the initial breach in the escarpment wall, the stream continues the process. Sands eroded from the mountaintops move downstream in the strong current. Rocky debris in and around the streambed attests to the creek's power. The stream course's main features are a series of powerful waterfalls and cascades.

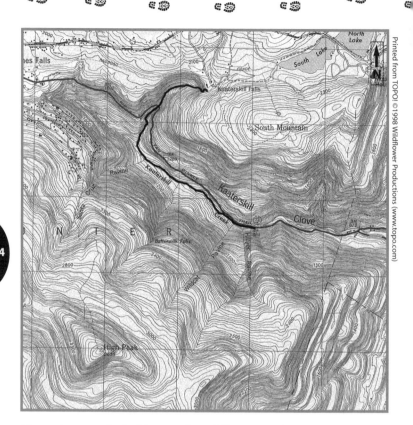

Throughout geologic history, these falls migrated upstream, carving ever deeper into the earth.

Upstream from Palenville, rapids and swimming holes fill Kaaterskill Creek's lower reaches. The cold, swift flowing waters rarely reach 65F degrees. Strong, fast currents produce distinctive features, including potholes and undercuts. Potholes form when a rock caught in a depression spins like a drill bit. Powered by the stream flow, the trapped rock grinds into the streambed to create the pothole. Eventually, the rock washes downstream or erodes, leaving a small circular hole. A few trout often call these potholes home.

The first major waterfall upstream from Palenville is Fawn's Leap. Racing down a vertical sandstone wall, the water drops 30 feet. Below its smooth, banked sides, the water fills a crystal-clear, 12-foot-deep pool. The fall's name arises from a local legend about a fawn's attempt to jump the chasm. Trapped by a hunter, the deer had no choice but to jump. The hunter watched the ill-fated leap and saw the fawn plunge into the icy waters.

Above Fawn's Leap, a small canyon constricts Kaaterskill Creek, while the clove's walls rise to towering heights. The road remains with the cliffs, abandoning the stream to the wilderness. Small rainbow and brook trout search for food in the pools. Deer come to drink the clear, cold water. Bears lounge in the midday sun. Hemlock trees spread their dark, feathery foliage to gather sunlight. Small plants and colorful wildflowers dance in the valley breezes.

Except in spring, or when waters are high, it is possible to climb the clove by following the stream course. Rocks, downed trees, and shorelines provide a random, yet dry route. Jumping from stone to stone is not a science. It is art. The mind must combine the intricacies of three dimensions and basic physics to determine the best path. Remaining dry is a constant challenge. Wet soles reduce traction and weigh down feet, causing additional slips, but in mid-summer heat the cool water often is a much-needed respite.

Stone hopping is a freestyle event. No correct form exists. Some dart from one submerged stone to another, while others carefully calculate the best course. Inner satisfaction is the only criteria, although waterlogged shoes often judge a jumping strategy's success.

The rocky streambed follows a moderate slope. Steep walls rise out of sight, seeming to fully enclose the clove. Along the clove's south wall a 40-foot cascade tumbles over soft red sandstones and into Kaaterskill Creek. The fall is a hanging valley, formed as glaciers enlarged the main valley faster than its tributaries.

Kaaterskill Clove's floor supports many plant species. Soft hemlocks line the streambank, thriving in the cool, damp environment. A northern hardwood forest, dominated by sugar maple, beech, and yellow birch, grow beyond the hemlocks. Warmer, drier sites support northern red oak. Gray squirrels and chipmunks love the acorns. In turn, these small mammals transport and plant the nuts. Beneath the lush forest grows a thick understory of jewelweed, stinging nettles, and grasses.

The rocks in and around the creek reveal the story of a waterfall. Almost every rock in the streambed once sat atop a waterfall. The falls migrated upstream, eroding the clove. Rushing water cracked, broke, and deepened the clove. As the falls eroded, pebbles, rocks, and boulders would litter the stream. Once in the water, the currents rounded and shaped these materials into their present forms.

Kaaterskill Creek splits three miles upstream from Palenville. The left fork, Kaaterskill Creek, leads to 180-foot Haines Falls. The right fork follows Lake Creek to Kaaterskill Falls, New York's highest waterfall. Upon following Lake Creek, the topography changes. Slopes steepen, and large boulders dominate the stream course. The spirited waters weave and dive through small pools and active cascades. Sheer rock walls close about the streambed. Unlike Kaaterskill Creek, Lake Creek's rocks are angular and blocky, still untamed by the flowing water. The water appears too busy to erode these rocks, yet the degradation exists—albeit at a slow pace. In time, if uninterrupted, erosion will level Lake Creek with the Hudson Valley.

Lake Creek continues to climb, eventually reaching Kaaterskill Clove's second major waterfall. Bastion Falls is a collection of falls, cascades, steep rock faces, and tumbling, roaring water. The Rip Van Winkle Trail, New York Route 23A, crosses the site. A concrete and steel bridge divides the falls in two, as man's reinforced structure trespasses over nature's splendor. Enhancing the falls popularity, yet leading to its deterioration, its position is a blessing and a curse. Hundreds of vehicles cross the falls daily, apathetically releasing nitrogen and hydrocarbon-laden exhaust. The fall's continuous spray of water valiantly struggles into the locally tainted air. Before the road passed these falls, they were popular with painters and conservationists. Despite the bridge and its traffic, Bastion Falls remains a pleasant, if not virgin, site.

Many thousands of travelers pass Bastion Falls as they motor on the Rip Van Winkle Trail, yet they miss one of the Catskills' most spectacular shows a half-mile upstream. A trail begins at the falls, following the stream to Kaaterskill Falls. Cold, rocky, and swift, Lake Creek makes a challenging route. The marked trail provides a drier, easier experience. Rock walls and forest become a collection of colors. Soft red shales and sandstones of the Oneonta formation mix with blocky, gray and greenish Hamilton sandstones. Dark hemlocks, red maple, yellow birch, and orange jewelweed surround the path.

Kaaterskill Clove's walls reveal the stream's natural history. Lake Creek erodes the western bank Grand Canyon-style. Devonian red beds mix with harder, younger sandstones. The steep eastern wall slips and slides into the stream.

A virgin hemlock grove surrounds Kaaterskill Fall's base; with trees 400 years old, this mature hemlock stand remained untouched during the leather tanning boom of the mid-1800s. The inaccessible clove prevented efficient transport, so loggers bypassed these trees. Once the Catskills' great hemlock stands no longer covered the mountains, the isolated stands became important to the tourist industry and America's young conservation movement.

The stream's roar deepens as the last bend brings Kaaterskill Falls into view, its 260-foot whitewater ribbon surging down the mountainside. The fall has two stages. The first leaps 180 feet into a large pool. Then the water jumps another 80 feet before ending as a series of cascades. Resistant Hamilton sandstones support the falls' protruding ledges. Softer red sandstones and shales erode faster, forming a cave behind the 180-foot drop. Horizontal rock platforms provide a small escarpment trail into the cavern. From its back wall, through the spray of water and beyond Kaaterskill Clove, Hunter Mountain dances along the skyline. The fall's lacy white curtain provided the inspiration for Thomas Cole's painting, *Kaaterskill Falls*.

A difficult and dangerous climb along the falls' western ledges (not part of the official trail) leads from bottom to top. A road from Haines Falls also accesses this crest. Perched on an open rock ledge, the top of Kaaterskill Falls is a nice place to relax. From a narrow spillway, Lake Creek's water continually begins its wild journey down Kaaterskill Clove.

The 80-foot lower tier of Kaaterskill Falls

Although forest covers the landscape around the falls, the area shows signs of its human past. Small pieces of coal lie on the ground. A railroad once ran to the area's resorts, and the tracks are still visible within the returning forest. Young stems cover most of the area. In the mid-1800s, a hotel, the Laurel House, stood near the falls. Named for the area's abundant mountain laurel, it became a popular resort. It was less prestigious than the nearby Catskill Mountain House and Hotel Kaaterskill, as it catered to the middle-class.

The owner of Kaaterskill Falls and the Laurel House capitalized on the local scenery. He placed a vending stand that served cool drinks and sweet snacks at the fall's summit. A large wooden staircase led down the mountainside so even the "ladies" could visit the bottom. The most profitable, and to many early conservationists, the most offensive undertaking was his alteration to the falls. He placed a small dam above the falls, to control water flow. By opening the dam, he could increase the volume to assembled crowds. With the area's economic decline, the dam fell to ruin, allowing the water to again flow unimpeded.

Winter brings a new dimension to Kaaterskill Falls. Ice columns grow when temperatures remain below freezing. Eventually the stream freezes. The ice grows as water spills over the fall, adding to the building ice dome. The brown-stained, milky ice sculpture celebrates winter's icy grip. The column can grow to 120 feet.

A trip up Kaaterskill Clove brings adventure and beauty in unspoiled wilderness. Water, in streams and waterfalls, is a constant companion over the clove's 2,000 vertical feet. Plants and animals continue their lifestyle in an ecosystem largely unchanged for 3,000 years. Frozen in time, the water's pace clocks a timeless world. A journey though the clove reveals this continuing story. It is one worth experiencing again and again.

HAINES FALLS

Kaaterskill Creek's waters never rest during their journey to the Hudson Valley. Racing waters constantly cascade over boulders and ledges lining the bottom of Kaaterskill Clove. Young and lively, the stream hammers at the unyielding sandstone bedrock. Small falls and large cascades of various notoriety lie all along this untamed watercourse. Kaaterskill Creek splits three miles upstream from Palenville, dividing its erosional power between two branches. Lake Creek, the northern fork, continues along South Mountain's eastern wall. Along this branch, two magnificent and well-known waterfalls, Bastion and Kaaterskill Falls, accelerate the water downstream.

Kaaterskill Creek's southern fork maintains a westerly course. After the split, water volume decreases and the streambed steepens. Angular boulders replace rounded rocks, and the main flow often leaps below these sandstone giants. The rushing water saturates the air with a dull roar. The surrounding area vibrates with the waters' power. Tapering stream channels pull the clove's walls close to the crystal waters. The hiker is without benefit of a streambank, and remaining dry while traveling upstream is a small miracle.

A set of lesser waterfalls and cascades add beauty and difficulty to the journey. The falls, one of well over a hundred feet, lie almost forgotten among the depths of Kaaterskill Clove. Hemmed by dangerous and steep cliffs, the final reaches of Kaaterskill Clove are beyond the skills of most humans; however, the stone barriers present little hindrance to the falling water. With a final upsurge through the canyon, the creekbed ascends Kaaterskill Clove's back wall. Before completing its journey, Kaaterskill Creek surges down Haines Falls.

Good eyes can discern the 180-foot waterfall from the Rip Van Winkle Trail (New York Route 23A). The falls appear as a frothy white line within the winter forest. The best of these views comes from the horseshoe curve downslope from Bastion Falls, but this miniature view does Haines Falls little justice.

Privately owned, Haines Falls has lost its fame of the 1800s. Nestled within the holdings of the Twilight Park Association, access is

Painted trillium

forbidden. State land leads partway up the clove above the junction of Kaaterskill and Lake Creeks, but the clove's head is private land.

Today Haines Falls plummets in relative obscurity. Still, the cultural loss of favor does not reduce its natural significance. Haines Falls exposes rock strata important in understanding Kaaterskill Clove's geology and geography. Set along the clove's western terminus, Haines Falls' geology mirrors that of Kaaterskill Falls.

Traversed by a small bridge, the fall's top roars close to civilization. Canyon walls pen the watercourse, and dense vegetation hides the majestic waterfall from view. In the mid-1800s, when the area was a prime summer retreat, wooden steps provided an easy trip along the waterfall. Time and neglect removed the stairs.

Haines Falls, in contrast with dual-tiered Kaaterskill Falls, is a single drop of 180 feet. A few hundred feet downstream, a rapid succession of falls and cascades drop the stream an additional few hundred feet. Haines Falls holds higher water volumes than Kaaterskill Falls, allowing it to carve deeper into the clove's back wall. Both falls plummet down layers of hard, gray Hamilton sandstones and soft, red-tinted Oneonta shales. The shales erode quickly, leaving sandstone overhangs. The resistant overhangs support the falls.

Haines Falls cuts through more Hamilton sandstones than Kaaterskill Falls. The rock strata are in transition. With less of the softer shales, the stream cuts its channel more slowly. The additional sandstone layers also provide additional support for the steep canyon walls. The relative strength of the Hamilton and Oneonta formations show in the area's ledges.

A waterfall's natural history is a constantly changing story. Former sandstone ledges, undermined long ago by eroded shales, litter Haines Falls' base. Large chunks of angular, gray-bronze sandstone lie in ruin. The broken rocks are a memorial to the waters' unyielding power. Many of these ledges were former plunge points for the waterfall. In contrast, the local sand and gravel derive from the rapidly eroding shales.

Haines Falls' plunge begins within a narrow rock crevice. Once it drops, the fall opens into a large natural amphitheater. Sheer sandstone cliffs and angled shale slopes bound the sheltered area. Walls to either side of the fall grow to enormous heights, their structures spared the water's onslaught. Despite the short-term reprieve, erosion takes its eventual toll. In time, these walls will collapse to continue the rocky, V-shaped valley taking shape downstream.

It is difficult to view Haines Falls in this landscape of high, curving, and vertical walls. The narrow, bending valley limits sight distance to a few hundred feet. Due to the narrow canyon and heavy vegetation, it is harder to photograph Haines Falls than Kaaterskill Falls.

Plant life includes species found throughout the clove, but the falls' extra moisture enhances local diversity. Beech, sugar maple, white pine, paper birch, and hemlock dominate the forest. Striped maple and beech saplings fill the canopy gaps, striving for a daily slice of sunlight. Ferns, mosses, and flowers ranging from jewelweed to trout lilies cover the forest floor. Green, slimy algae colonies coat the cold, wet rock walls.

Hemlocks thrive on the damp slopes surrounding the waterfall. Their dark, thick foliage intercepts incoming sunlight, helping maintain the cool, damp environment. Despite the excellent habitat, most local hemlocks are small. Steep local topography prevents soil accumulation, so large trunks easily uproot.

Winter is a time of rest and icy beauty around Haines Falls. Life's pulse ebbs and summer's torrent quiets to winter's trickles. The water flow, caught behind ice dams and frozen pools, slows. Drop by drop, Kaaterskill Creek freezes in place. Sunny days free some of the water, sending it from sun to shade as it descends. When it cools, the water often freezes on the giant ice columns forming at the fall's base. The column can grow to 120 feet high and 50 feet in diameter. On the shaded, north-facing cliffs bordering the waterfall, ice crystalizes into large pillars. Some columns tint with the dusty red of iron oxide, while other pillars are blue from dissolved methane. Shapes, colors, and textures form ice gardens, with each year its own unique show.

Haines Falls stands atop Kaaterskill Creek, its waters carving the clove's western half. The falls are the start of a wild journey to the Hudson River, 2,000 feet below. Although no longer a popular landmark, Haines Falls retains its beauty.

ROUNDTOP

Hike: Roundtop
Roundtrip Hiking Distance: varies based on approach
    and route to snowmobile trail (from 5-12 miles)
County and Town: Greene, Hunter
Parking: (best access) Off Platte Clove Road,
    (on south side of road, just east of stone bridge)
    Trail is on north side of road
Difficulty: difficult
Bushwhack: yes (minimum .8 miles, depending on route)
Elevation Gain: (from parking area on Platte Clove Road) 1450 feet
    (begin due west of Roundtop along the snowmobile trail—the
    Snowmobile trail can be accessed via the route used to
    approach Kaaterskill High Peak)
Mile: 0.0: Leave snowmobile trail, begin bushwhack up the mountain
    0.4: Reach summit of Roundtop, end of trip

The sun makes an early appearance to one perched atop Roundtop. As the glowing orb rises above the distant Taconic Hills, it bathes the summer landscape with warm tones. Tendrils of early morning fog slip from the Hudson Valley toward the mountain heights. Carefully, they work into the depths of Platte Clove and caress the mountain forests. The ephemeral cloud pulls the eye into the mountains. In the saddle below, a lighter-colored forest blankets the land. The dark, foreboding bulk of Kaaterskill High Peak dominates the foreground. Strong, straight trunks tell the brave story of the spruce-fir forest capping the summit. A huge drop separates the overlook from the isolated mountain and thick forest, yet the spirit yearns to span the gap and meld with the glorious scene. The eye leaves this sunrise scene along a wide bend in the Hudson River, the uplifting landscape filling the new day with beauty and inspiration.

So depicts Thomas Cole, founder of the Hudson River School of Landscape Painting, in his work, *Sunny Morning on the Hudson River*. The picture is an event repeated daily on Roundtop Mountain, the inspiration for this piece. Unlike most of the Catskills' historic landscapes, this one still lives in wilderness.

Roundtop Mountain, when viewed from Kaaterskill Clove's steep slopes, towers high above the rugged landscape. Each spring, its sharp peak remains buried in snow long after the surrounding cloves grow green in May's warmth. On Roundtop's lower slopes, man's dominion invades its forests. Twilight Park and Cortina Valley ski center cover Roundtop's northwestern face, dividing soaring mountain from cascading clove.

Steep ravines, another product of recent glaciation, rush into Katerskill Clove. Energetic streams from Roundtop tumble down the steep mountain faces. Most race down sharp cliffs and small waterfalls. Some drop more than 100 feet in a single plunge. The land is wild and often inaccessible.

Beautiful lookouts over Kaaterskill Clove open from Roundtop's northern face. Located off-trail, these ledges overlook the clove to unveil vistas of North Mountain, Stoppel Point, and the massive Blackhead Range. The famous lookout from the mountaintop provides a beautiful view of the Hudson Valley. Thomas Cole and the other painters of the Hudson River School brought these views to millions of people throughout the world.

Roundtop, at 3,440, feet is among the Catskills' 50 highest peaks; however, its eastern neighbor, 3,655-foot Kaaterskill High Peak often eclipses it. Roundtop and Kaaterskill High Peak rise on the same sandstone base, towering above the eastern escarpment and the Hudson Valley. From the east and west, Kaaterskill High Peak swallows Roundtop's lower form. When viewed from the north and south, the two isolated peaks are a pair of waves forever about to crash onto the Hudson Valley.

Together, Kaaterskill High Peak and Roundtop compose a mountain island. Separated from other peaks by the Schoharie Valley and the deep Kaaterskill and Platte Cloves, Roundtop's sharp, distinctive shape makes it an imposing landform. The Schoharie's headwaters merge with runoff from

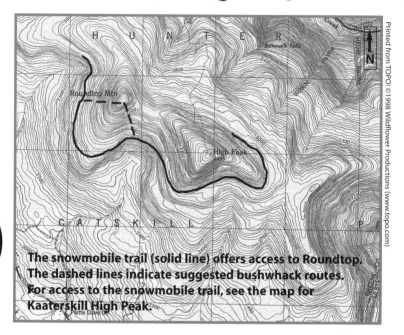

The snowmobile trail (solid line) offers access to Roundtop. The dashed lines indicate suggested bushwhack routes. For access to the snowmobile trail, see the map for Kaaterskill High Peak.

Roundtop's drainage. East of Kaaterskill High Peak, the steep drop into the Hudson Valley provides another sharp topographical contrast.

No trails lead to Roundtop's summit, yet it is not difficult to reach. A snowmobile trail encircles Kaaterskill High Peak and Roundtop at 3,100 feet. Often waterlogged because of its location on a poorly drained, flat ledge, the trail typifies glaciated terrain. Impeded by fragipans, water collects along the trail, escaping only by evaporation. One result is that feet often sink six inches or more into the muddy terrain.

Below the glacial landscape, resistant horizontal layers of Hamilton sandstone support the ledge. Despite the trail's rigors, it offers rewards. Animal tracks, including deer, fox, and bear, are common in the muddy causeway.

The snowmobile trail provides easy access to Roundtop's summit. The easiest is from the western and southern faces. Just go up.

Roundtop's western face has no disorienting false peaks, towering cliffs, or sharp drops. The southern face is a bit steeper, but no more difficult. Easy-to-find-and-follow deer trails crisscross the mountain. Forest cover thins as elevation reaches 3,300 feet. Winds pick up, and glimpses of the surrounding mountains slip through small gaps in the forest canopy.

Wildflowers and other flora abound on Roundtop's undisturbed slopes. Purple trillium, foamflower, white snakeroot, jack-in-the-pulpit, white baneberry, and a host of other colored beauties decorate the mountainside. Stinging nettles monopolize large patches, one of the largest engulfing the snowmobile trail.

Stinging nettles are among the forest's greatest menaces. Their prey are often unsuspecting humans wearing shorts. When touched, stems covered with small and harmless looking hairs slip into the skin. The painless insertion draws no blood. The contact pressure causes the hollow thorn to react as a hypodermic needle. Its contents, formic acid, are injected into the victim. Formic acid is also an active ingredient in bee stings and ant bites. The hundreds of tiny doses result in mild streaks of fiery pain. Scratching, which dulls the body's nervous system, is the only effective physical treatment. The pain subsides within a few very-long-seeming minutes; however, there is a faster herbal remedy. The sap of jewelweed, also called touch-me-not, counteracts formic acid. Finding some is the biggest problem. Although common, and often growing in the same vicinity as stinging nettle, like a police officer, it is never there when needed. Stinging nettles also begin to grow earlier in the season, making the task of finding the antidote almost impossible in May.

As the bushwhack up Roundtop's western face continues, the forest of birch, beech, and maple trees shrinks. Hobblebush, ferns and grasses—many dry and brown—dominate the undergrowth. Although the slopes moderate as the mountaintop nears, the summit remains elusive. Then, without warning, one reaches the small, flat peak. Blueberries, red spruce, and balsam fir cover the mountaintop. Flagged trees record the constant westerly winds.

Roundtop's small summit is a level parcel of rocky ground surrounded by sharp drops to the north and south. A sheer cliff lines its eastern face. The peak supports a spruce-fir forest, and the sweet smell of balsam scents the air. Small, stunted hardwoods, mostly pin cherry and birch, join sprawling, entangling hobblebush and mountain maple. Open meadows, maintained by high winds, harsh conditions, and even an occasional small fire, complete Roundtop's vegetational community.

Roundtop's history is long and unique among the Catskills. Tories and their Iroquois allies used it as a lookout post and holding area for rebellious colonists during the American Revolution. They built a small fort 500 feet below the summit. The peak commands a wide view of the Hudson Valley, which provided an excellent place to observe troop movements. Secluded and well guarded, the Loyalists' base stood unchallenged. Besides the fort's strategic importance, it secured open communications and supply lines for British forces to the west. Traces of the fort and its foundation remain on the mountain's southern face.

The strategic and scenic eastern overlook remains unobstructed by vegetation. Kaaterskill High Peak rises in the foreground, dominating the eastern sky. The land between the two peaks falls quickly to form a sea of air between the mountaintops. The 300-foot drop is only a step away. Slices of the placid Hudson River slip through the steep openings of Kaaterskill and Platte Cloves. Nestled along the Hudson to the southeast is historic Kingston, first capital of New York. To the northeast, and a thousand feet below this perch, are North and South Lakes and the Pine Orchard, site of the Catskill Mountain House, lying atop the eastern escarpment. In spring, perky cornusberry flowers decorate this overlook, while late summer provides tasty blueberries.

Roundtop also provides a panoramic western view, encompassing the northern Catskills. From Sugarloaf Mountain to the south, to the mighty Blackheads to the north, this vista encompasses more than 30 major Catskill peaks. The modest, bubbled form of Clum Hill occupies the western foreground and is the third peak on this small mountain island. Behind Clum Hill rises heavily-glaciated Onteora Mountain and the East Jewett Range. Between these low peaks and Clum Hill, Rip Van Winkle Lake shimmers in the sunlight. Tannersville lies north of the lake.

Looking south from Roundtop's summit—Twin Mountain

Sugarloaf Mountain, to the south, marks the midpoint of the Devil's Path, a rugged ridgeline cutting the Catskills in two. Sprucetop Mountain juts from its northern slopes, bearing toward Roundtop. West of Sugarloaf, the Devil's Path falls into Mink Hollow and then lifts to build Plateau Mountain. Through Mink Hollow are the distant peaks of the Burroughs Range: Wittenberg, Cornell, Friday, and Balsam Cap Mountains. After tracing Plateau's long, flat summit, the land drops into Stony Clove before climbing 4,040-foot Hunter Mountain, the Catskills' second highest peak. The fire tower topping Hunter's massive slopes pokes above its summit vegetation. Northwest of Hunter is a slice of Rusk Mountain. Within the space carved by Stony Clove rises 4,180-foot Slide Mountain, the Catskills' highest peak. Its hazy form silently reminds Hunter which mountain is king of the Catskills.

The Schoharie Creek and Valley separate Roundtop and the nearby Devil's Path Mountains. Some of the Catskills' prominent 19th-cen-

A view of Kaaterskill High Peak from the summit of Roundtop

tury visitors loved the flowing valleys so much they commented that the mountains seemed to exist for the sole purpose of beautifying these wide and scenic valleys. When traveling in the easily accessible stream valleys and looking up at the mountain, it is hard to argue otherwise; however, when perched atop Roundtop's spectacular summit, this perspective becomes difficult to accept, the opposite seeming the more likely truth.

THE DEVIL'S PATH

The mountains crossed by the Devil's Path compose one of the Catskills' highest ridgelines. The path runs east-west over six mountains: Indian Head, Twin, Sugarloaf, Plateau, Hunter, and Westkill Mountains; however, New York Route 214 runs between Plateau and Hunter Mountains, separating Hunter and Westkill Mountains from their eastern brothers. The separation limits modern associations. For this reason, Hunter and Westkill Mountains are explored in other sections of this book.

Along the Devil's Path, rugged terrain is the rule. Sharp cliffs, steep trails, impassable forests, and spectacular vistas populate the range. The four eastern peaks—Indian Head, Twin, Sugarloaf, and Plateau—define a wilderness area.

Looking south at Guardian and Tonche Mountains from Jimmy Dolan Notch

Henry Hudson, sailing for the Dutch, first entered the river now bearing his name. His ship, *Half Moon*, sailed upriver looking for a passage to the Orient. He and his crew provided the first written description Europeans made of the Catskill Mountains; their foreboding peaks rose within a few miles of the wide, placid river.

The Dutch were the first Europeans to settle the Mid-Hudson Valley in the 1600s. They farmed the fertile valleys and built small trading towns. The Catskills' dark, watchful peaks rose west of the settlements. The Dutch believed that evil spirits, witches, and terrible beasts lived among the wild heights. Except for a few brave hunters and trappers, the Dutch avoided the mountains. The names given the timeless peaks often reflect this early reputation. The Devil's Path, a Catskill range in southern Greene County, is one example

The State-marked trail (aptly identified with red markers) runs undisturbed over this ridge, providing an extensive wilderness adventure. Starting from Prediger Road, the Devil's Path climbs Indian Head Mountain. After the trail traverses Twin, Sugarloaf, and Plateau Mountains, it bisects Route 214 in Stony Clove. Even after 350 years of western civilization, the Devil's Path remains a simple dirt trail over rugged terrain. The land is still wilderness.

The Devil's Path Mountains are characterized by steep eastern faces, flat-topped mountains, and cliff-like drops on western slopes; hiking these mountains taxes legs and knees. Notches separating the mountains provide access to the peaks. They were the main passages through the mountains before the railroad era. The notches—Jimmy Dolan, Pecoy, Mink Hollow, and Stony Clove—make good hikes themselves. A campground, Devil's Tombstone, nestles in Stony Clove.

Glaciation played an important role in the Catskills' recent geological history. The mountains steered ice flows south and east through the Schoharie Valley. As the continental ice sheets advanced, they slammed into the Devil's Path. Notches formed where ice broke the mountain wall. From west to east, each successive notch bites less severely into the ridge. As the climate warmed, glacial lakes formed in the plugged Schoharie Valley. The notches were the waters' first escape.

Constricted into these small outlets, the glacial lakes flowed through these notches with tremendous force.

The massive amounts of glacial meltwaters created a torrent of erosion, enlarging notches and stream valleys. As the ice further retreated, the water found new, lower exits. The meltwaters scoured Stony Clove more than its neighboring notches. Deepest and westernmost of the Devil's Path notches, Stony Clove lies only 2,010 feet above sea level. Mink Hollow is next, separating Plateau and Sugarloaf at 2,600 feet. Pecoy Notch sits between Sugarloaf and Twin Mountains at 2,900 feet. The rugged 3,110-foot Jimmy Dolan Notch lies between Twin and Indian Head Mountains.

INDIAN HEAD

Hike: Indian Head
Circuit Hiking Distance: 6.1 miles
County and Town: Greene, Hunter
Parking: Southern terminus of Prediger Road, off Platte Clove Road
Difficulty: difficult
Bushwhack: no
Elevation Gain: 1575 feet
Mile 0.0: Trail begins at terminus of Prediger Road
     (red markers)
    0.4: Junction with Jimmy Dolan Trail (blue markers)
    2.0: Reach Jimmy Dolan Notch and turn east on Devil's Path Trail.
    2.5: Pass summit of Indian Head
    2.9: Reach excellent viewpoints to eastern (lower) peak
    4.5: Devil's Path turns west
    5.6: Rejoin the Jimmy Dolan Notch Trail at its lower terminus
    6.1: Return to parking area on Prediger Road

Indian Head rises 3,573 feet above sea level, anchoring the Devil's Path's eastern end. Accessible from the slopes bounding Platte Clove, this distinctive mountain reflects its name. The Ashokan Reservoir is an excellent place to view the Indian's profile.

The Devil's Path begins along the Schoharie's headwater valleys. The trail winds onto Indian Head's eastern slopes, passing through mixed forests of northern hardwoods and hemlock. The trail climbs a small ridge before turning west to ascend the mountain. After crossing a series of small stream valleys, it continues through typical Catskill forests. Small, dark hemlock groves contrast with brighter deciduous stands. The sound of softly flowing water fades as the trail begins a steeper ascent.

The path surges into Indian Head's upper elevations along a series of steep slopes and switchbacks. Loose rocks tile the ground. Layers of sandstones and shale build the mountain's heights. The higher elevations introduce harsher conditions that affect forest growth. A transition zone forest of yellow birch, paper birch, striped maple, mountain maple, sugar maple, black cherry, American beech, and balsam fir cover the mountainside. Breezes roll through the forest, swaying trees and cooling the air. Hints of balsam perfume the mountainsides. The climbing continues until the trail opens onto an extensive vista overlooking Platte Clove. Kaaterskill High Peak and Roundtop line the clove's northern wall. Northwest of these peaks rise the Blackhead range, the northern Catskills' highest summits.

Indian Head's eastern slopes are steep. Two of the Catskills' past economic engines line the trail: hemlock trees and bluestone. Muted and calm, the serene hemlock groves contrast with the brighter northern hardwood forests. Large, dark hemlocks, some more than 250 years old, dominate the forest. Except for bronze carpets of fallen needles, the forest floor is bare. Soils are soft and dark, muffling footsteps and enhancing shadows. Few flowers grow. Direct sunlight rarely reaches the ground. Small sounds tread warily amid the thick silence. An edgy air of anticipation saturates the grove. Many forests older and larger than these stands covered wide areas of the Catskills until the 1850s.

Shrouded in darkness and silence, and populated with the worst specters of man's imagination, it is no surprise that early European settlers shunned the Catskills. Local Indians also created many legends about the mountains. But around 1820, people finally moved into the area, cutting the hemlocks for their tannin content. The bark provided a cheap source of leather-making chemicals. Large tanneries opened in the Catskills, and in less than 50 years the old-growth hemlock forests lay in ruin.

Excellent examples of bluestone lie along the trail. Catskill bluestones are shales, deposited along an ancient coastline 350 million years ago. Above the hemlock grove, exposed bedrock splits into horizontal layers. The natural formation appears the work of an expert stonecutter. Bluestone made the Catskills famous in the late nineteenth century. It faced buildings, paved city streets, and lined sidewalks. Fueled by the northeast's expanding cities, demand for paving stones grew, and the Catskills had the best supply. But without a large investment to determine quality, a quarry's value remained uncertain. Speculators

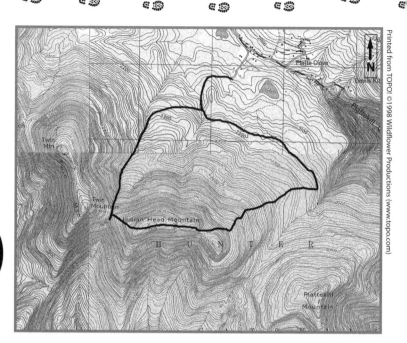

made and lost fortunes looking for quality deposits. When Portland cement developed in the late 1890s, it made bluestone obsolete. Bluestone boomtowns, including West Hurley and Phoenicia, faced economic collapse. The last major project to use bluestone was the Ashokan Reservoir. Quarries now flooded by its waters provided the rock lining its basin.

Indian Head's vistas are among the Catskills' best. Awe-inspiring views open in two places along the mountain's top ridge. A third over-look, a few hundred feet off-trail, provides another breathtaking vista. When moving along the Indian's profile from east to west, the first view opens after topping the Indian's chin. The southwest facing view overlooks the central and southern Catskills. Overlook Mountain lines the panoramic scene's southeastern fringe. Its sandstone backbone gen-tly falls north and west, melding into its western neighbor, Guardian Mountain.

Although impressive from the surrounding valleys, the 3,150-foot Overlook Mountain falls into perspective when viewed from its higher relations. The Ashokan Reservoir fills the Esopus Basin, its waters reflecting the moods of sky, mountain, and earth varying in color from brown and gray to blue and green. Beyond the artificial lake rises 3,098-foot Ashokan High Point. Behind this three-tiered mountain and the Rondout Creek's underfit valley are the Shawangunks. Their sharp ridgeline slices to the southwest, falling behind the southern Catskills.

The Catskills' central high peaks lift west of the reservoir. Peekamoose and Table Mountains sharpen the southwestern background. The Burroughs Range is next, a series of summits rising from the reservoir's western shore. Highest among them is Slide Mountain, king of the Catskills. North of Slide, a high ridge melds into Giant Ledge before cresting as Panther Mountain's 3,720-foot peak. Big Indian, Eagle, Fir, Doubletop, Graham, and Balsam Lake Mountains stretch to the western horizon.

After a quick descent and then a short, steep climb, a flat, pock-marked ledge reveals a second vista. Perched atop Indian Head's nose, this east view overlooks the Indian's chin. The small ledge invites the passerby to sit and reflect on nature's grandeur. On a clear, low-pollution day, this view ranks among the Catskills' best. It is a place of peace; the mind is free to soar with hawks and eagles. Time passes swiftly. To the northeast, the wilds of Platte Clove slice the escarpment wall. Overlook and Guardian Mountains stand in the southeast. Beyond Overlook, Kingston sits in the charming Mid-Hudson Valley. The Ashokan Reservoir, Ashokan High Point, Tycetonyk Mountain, and the Shawangunks fill the southwest. Hundreds of thousands of acres of unspoiled mountain beauty unfold from this beautiful spot.

Indian Head's distinctive shape produces false summits, which can make it difficult to confirm the true peak. Careful observation and maps, however, reveal it as the last rise before descending into Jimmy Dolan Notch.

The summit supports a dense, healthy spruce-fir forest, a jungle of needles and branches. Many large, dead red spruce spear the sky. Bleached trunks, stripped of bark, loom like exposed mountain bones.

A southeastern view from one of Indian Head's open ledges—Indian Head's eastern knob and Overlook Mountain

Scientific and political debates surround the cause of death. Some argue acid rain is responsible, while others blame climate change, old age, or disease. The answer remains unclear. Perhaps a combination of factors are responsible. Whatever the reason, the spruce have made a comeback, confirmed by the hordes of saplings replacing the decaying giants.

A third vista opens on the summit's western slope. Located above Jimmy Dolan Notch, this small rock ledge peers west. A short, often soggy bushwhack through hobblebush, matted grasses, balsam fir, and assorted birch lead to the ledge. The overlook is south of the trail, at an elevation of 3,300 feet. It perches on a large sandstone outcropping protruding from the glacial till. After parting a final curtain of balsam fir, the ledge appears and the western horizon opens from north to south. Twin Mountain dominates the foreground, its sharp untamed cliffs rising across Jimmy Dolan Notch. Its steep eastern face mirrors Indian Head's difficult terrain. Far to the north, the Blackheads, Parker

Hill, Onteora Mountain, North Mountain, and Windham High Peak outline this scene. Tannersville and Rip Van Winkle Lake inhabit the Schoharie Valley. To the south is a copy of the view revealed from Indian Head's eastern slopes, but the foreground enhances this spectacular overlook. The rock ledge feels suspended in air. Jagged edges and large rocks speckle the terrain.

A fast, rugged, 460-foot drop from Indian Head's summit brings the trail into Jimmy Dolan Notch. Small cliffs, repeated switchbacks, loose stone, protruding roots, and tricky rock formations define the challenging trip. A few glimpses of Twin Mountain and the Blackheads peek through the thick forest cover. When looking at Indian Head's retreating summit, the steep profile confirms the difficult journey.

The slopes level off as the trail enters 3,110-foot Jimmy Dolan Notch. To the north a trail leads to Prediger Road, completing a six and a half mile loop on Indian Head Mountain. All the notches along the Devil's Path have side trails descending into adjoining valleys. Day hikes often include these trails.

A northern hardwood forest, mainly striped maple, mountain maple, mountain-ash, paper birch, and yellow birch, grows in the notch, while thick tangles of hobblebush line the forest floor. Large boulders from Indian Head and Twin's slopes line the gap. A short, unmarked spur trail leads south to a viewpoint overlooking the Catskills' eastern edge, including Guardian Mountain, the Sawkill Valley, and Ashokan High Point.

TWIN

Hike: Twin
Roundtrip Hiking Distance: 5.4 miles
County and Town: Greene, Hunter
Parking: Southern terminus of Prediger Road, off Platte Clove Road
Difficulty: moderate-difficult
Bushwhack: no
Elevation Gain: 1680 feet
Mile 0.0: Trail begins at terminus of Prediger Road
    0.1: Pass sign-in box
    0.5: Turn onto Jimmy Dolan Notch Trail (blue markers)
    1.6: Trail turns sharply west and begins a steep ascent
    2.0: Jimmy Dolan Notch; turn west up Twin (red markers)
    2.3: Pass small east-facing ledge
    2.4: Open panoramic ledge, summit of lower peak
    2.6: Summit of Twin
    2.7: West-facing ledge, return by same route
    3.4: Return to Jimmy Dolan Notch
    5.4: Return to parking area on Prediger Road

On the west side of Jimmy Dolan Notch, the Devil's Path begins its approach to Twin Mountain. Its challenging, almost vertical eastern slopes lie straight ahead and weigh heavily on tired muscles and spirits; however, instead of climbing the eastern face, the path mercifully veers northeast. Now part of the eastern skyline, Indian Head's mass looms beyond Twin's foliage. The trail clambers over sandstone boulders, small cliff faces, and tree roots. Handholds often ease the ascent. Sharp rock fragments trace the twisting, climbing route.

The coarse sandstone is more than 350 million years old, many of the boulders splitting from the parent bedrock during the cool period following glaciation. Freezing and thawing episodes weaken rock. Cracks formed and widened. Water seeped into the rocks. The process accelerated. Boulders broke and fell, many tumbling down the mountainside. Although randomly oriented, the sandstone's parallel cross-bedding is clear.

As elevation increases, the Catskills' characteristic stair-step topography becomes apparent. Wide openings reveal impressive views of Indian Head Mountain and the Hudson Valley. Environmental differences also denote the altitude gain. Forest composition changes. Balsam fir populate the forest along with paper birch and mountain-ash. Mountain maple and striped maple disappear. Yellow birch and hobblebush continue their presence. Characteristics of both communities mark this transition between northern hardwood and spruce-fir forests.

The transition zone forest is a distinct Catskill community. It occupies the space between bordering forest types, yet differs from its neighboring forests. Unable to produce a uniform canopy, it appears messy and unkempt. Stems and limbs litter the forest floor. Sunlight reaches the ground, so hobblebush, blackberries, and grasses thrive. Tall trees are rare. Within the Catskills, this transition zone forest usually occurs between 3,000 and 3,400 feet.

Winds increase, while temperature decreases, at higher elevations. The mountainous terrain encourages gusty conditions as valley bottoms and mountain summits heat and cool at different rates. In unmoving air, the temperature drops an average of 4F degrees for each 1,000 feet of elevation gain. The terrain and temperature gradients generate air flows from warm spots to cool ones. Sometimes the wind is a gentle breeze, but at others they reach gale force. Flag trees, one-sided trees, and broken limbs are common. Sunny days can produce 25F degree differences between the mountains and valleys. Cloudy days produce smaller temperature gradients and less wind. Local topography modifies these effects. On sunny days, southern slopes warm the most. Sheltered valleys often cool faster and for longer periods than neighboring heights. Since cold air sinks and the valleys lose the sun's warming rays before the mountains, a pool of cold air can collect in the valley bottoms. If a wind does not develop to mix the air, it will continue to cool and result in temperatures well below those on adjoining mountaintops. Record cold temperatures usually occur in valley bottoms, not on mountaintops.

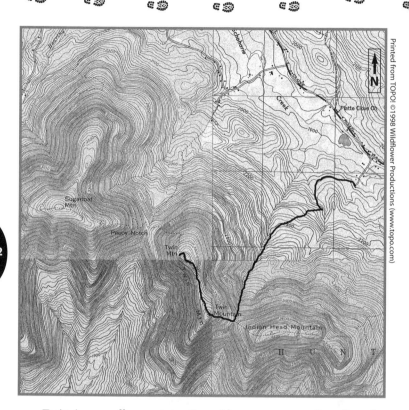

Twin is a small mountain. Few ridges or spurs radiate from its mass. The eastern peak rises to 3,580 feet, and it is an easy hike. The 400-foot climb from notch to crest moves quickly. Above 3,500 feet, a spruce-fir forest blankets the ground. Yellow birch, paper birch, and mountain-ash complete local tree diversity. The harsh conditions limit tree height to about 15 feet.

After passing the 3,500-foot mark, the path heads south. A small forest break and sandstone ledge peer east. Indian Head's summit rises across Jimmy Dolan Notch. Wearing a dark cap of spruce and fir, its top ridge sharply contrasts with the brighter green deciduous leaves. Its southern face, among the Catskills' steepest slopes, plunges into the

Sawkill Valley. Platte Clove bounds Indian Head's northern face. The Hudson River lies beyond its tumbling slopes. Exposed rock ledges on the clove's northeast edge define Huckleberry Point. On the eastern horizon is Mount Everett in northwestern Massachusetts. South of Indian Head is Overlook Mountain, its 3,150-foot form dwarfed by Indian Head and Twin. Marked by its 300-foot television tower, Overlook is easy to find.

Twin's eastern summit passes quickly. As the trail curls northwest, a 200-degree panoramic vista opens. Scrubby vegetation hems the windswept view's northern flank. Among the Catskills' far-reaching scenic views, this southwest-centered vista rates among the best. Overlook Mountain anchors the southeast, partially eclipsed by Twin's eastern slopes. The Shawangunks and Mid-Hudson Valley fill the southeast. Smaller Catskill peaks fill the southwestern foreground: Tremper, Tobias, Tonche, Carl, Pleasant, and Tycetonyk. They line the Esopus Valley's path through the mountains. Heavily dissected by glaciation, none of these peaks reaches 3,000 feet. South of the Ashokan Reservoir are Ashokan High Point, Rose, and Little Rocky Mountains. The massive Burroughs Range lifts west of these rounded slopes. Giant Ledge and Panther are north of Slide Mountain, the Catskills' highest point. Farther west is the long, high ridge upholding Belleayre with it scar-like ski trails, Balsam, Haynes, Eagle, Big Indian, and Fir Mountains. Behind this set soar Doubletop, Graham, and Balsam Lake Mountains. The foreground mountains—Olderbark, Plateau, Hunter, and neighboring Sugarloaf—add texture to the distant mountain patchwork. A slice of 3,380-foot Sprucetop juts into the northeastern view. Twin's western summit, 80 feet higher than its companion, lies northwest.

Once past the vista, the thin trail plunges into a thick spruce-fir forest. In late summer, ripe blueberries coat much of the ground. It is easy to reach the small notch separating Twin's peaks. Spruce and fir yield to yellow birch, mountain-ash, and paper birch. Mountain maple returns to the forest, then exits as the trail climbs again. The walk to the Twin's western summit is no harder than the short descent. The summit is quiet and secluded, submerged in the spruce-fir forest.

Looking west from Twin's eastern summit toward its higher western summit

The soils topping Twin's higher elevations are a thin layer of black humus over bedrock. Poorly drained by the horizontal, impermeable sandstones, muck and mud soak the trail. Sustained and supported by only a few inches of wet soil, trees in this alpine forest rarely reach 20 feet. A vigorous tree will meet an early death in this wind-ravaged environment. Here, it is a disadvantage to grow too well.

Once beyond Twin's western summit, a slight descent brings the trail to another panoramic view. Poised westward, this vista unveils a landscape similar to Twin's other open ledge, but trades the southeast prospective for a northwest vantage including Huntersfield Mountain and the Catskills' northeastern escarpment. Sugarloaf Mountain fills the foreground. Barren, gray landslide scars paint its southeastern face. Behind it, Hunter Mountain's 80-foot fire tower juts from near its 4,040-foot summit. The U-shaped valleys and inverted U-shaped mountains reveal their glacial facelifts.

After the vista, the Devil's Path quickly descends 800 feet into Pecoy Notch. Numerous switchbacks aid the trail as it tours a cross section of Devonian rocks. As elevation decreases, the climate warms. A northern hardwood forest again dominates the slopes.

SUGARLOAF

Hike: Sugarloaf
Roundtrip Hiking Distance: 4.6 miles
County and Town: Greene, Hunter
Parking: Along Elka Park Road (about 1 mile from eastern junction with Platte Clove Road)
Difficulty: moderate-difficult
Bushwhack: no
Elevation Gain: 1850 feet
Mile: 0.0: Trail begins from small parking area along Elka Park Road (yellow markers)
0.3: Trail end; veer east (blue markers)
2.0: Pecoy Notch, turn west (right) to ascend Sugarloaf (red markers)
3.0: Summit of Sugarloaf
3.8: Spur trail leads to open, south-facing ledge, return by same route
4.2: Return to Pecoy Notch
5.9: Trail ends, follow yellow-marked trail
6.2: Return to Elka Park Road

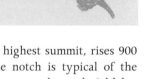

Sugarloaf Mountain, the Catskills 13th highest summit, rises 900 feet from the 2,900-foot Pecoy Notch. The notch is typical of the Catskills. From the underfit Schoharie Valley, once a large glacial lake, steep slopes rise to meet the mountains.

A spur trail with good views and beautiful forest stands leads into Pecoy Notch from Elka Park Road. It travels through a forest dominated by beech and sugar maple. Other local trees include paper birch, yellow birch, black cherry, northern red oak, and white pine. Hemlocks grow along the cool, damp streambanks. Flowers, including spring beauties, purple trillium, downy yellow violets, Canada violets, trout lilies, and bedstraws, colonize sun-flecked trailsides.

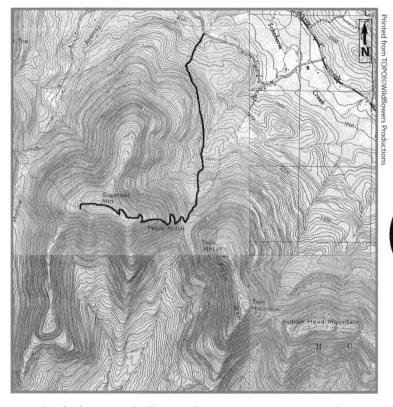

The climb to Sugarloaf's 3,800-foot summit is steep. Even the most sturdy hiker will feel winded after a few hundred feet. Twin Mountain, to the east, looms as a giant monolith. Twin rises to 3,680 feet, and its 780-foot rise above Pecoy Notch provides a benchmark for monitoring elevation. When looking at Twin with a stick held horizontally at eye level, it estimates elevation relative to the mountaintop and the notch bottom.

A few views peer south and southeast from small cliffs and switchbacks. Overlook Mountain squats to the east, appearing much lower from this vantage than from the Hudson Valley or Woodstock. Good views of the Ashokan Reservoir also open from these small ledges. The

A view east toward Twin Mountain

difficult climb then continues, moderating once reaching the gently rounded summit. A dense spruce-fir forest shepherds the trail through the harsh terrain. The true peak passes unceremoniously as the trail tumbles over tangled roots and through soggy soils.

South of the summit, a spur trail leads to an open viewpoint placed atop sandstone ledges. The ground plummets into the Sawkill Valley, accenting this open perch. Centered southward, the vista takes in the Hudson Valley, Ashokan Reservoir, and the central Catskill peaks. Olderbark Mountain, a sandstone and shale wall rising to 3,440 feet, fills the western view. Mt. Tobias, Mt. Pleasant, Mt. Tremper, and Tycetonyk Mountain stand the middle ground, north and east of the reservoir. Guardian Mountain spills from Overlook Mountain, its profile leading south into Cooper Lake. When sun-baked, this warm ledge often removes the nip from a cool day.

Descending Sugarloaf is tricky. Its western face thrusts ledge after ledge through the trail. In winter and early spring, tricky slopes become treacherous. The trail follows a small streambed and freezes into a vertical sheet of ice. Freezes and thaws glaze the Devil's Path's western slopes. A slip on these icy slopes can result in a 30-foot drop. Winter hiking along the eastern and northern faces usually makes for safer treks.

After descending through 1,200 feet of cliffs, warming temperatures, and larger forests, the trail enters Mink Hollow. A lush and thriving northern hardwood forest fills the hollow. Cross-trails lead north and south from the lowpoint. About 8 miles long, the trail connects points 45 miles distant by paved road. The shorter, easier walk leads north. An old roadbed, the trail leads through forest lands quickly becoming homesites. Logging operations continue to convert maturing forest into open fields, and civilization soon follows.

Mink Hollow's name derives from the large mink population once living in the area. Local trappers at first bought furs from the Indians, then later trapped the animals themselves. Maps from the mid-1800s label Sugarloaf Mountain "Mink Mountain." Almost extirpated from the area in the 1800s, mink remain rare.

PLATEAU

Hike: Plateau
Roundtrip Hiking Distance: 5.2 miles
County and Town: Greene, Hunter
Parking: Devil's Tombstone camping area, along Route 214 in Stony Clove
Difficulty: difficult
Bushwhack: no
Elevation Gain: 1800 feet
Mile: 0.0: Stony Clove (red markers)(2.5 miles south of NY Route 23A on
     NY Route 214)
    0.6: Pass large rock slides
    1.0: Orchard Ledge; trail reaches long, level summit
    2.6: Summit of Plateau; return by same route
    4.2: Return to Orchard Ledge
    5.2: Return to Stony Clove

Mink Hollow's western slopes merge into Plateau Mountain. Stony Clove, the Devil's Path's deepest notch, is on the far side of this long, flat mountain. Either notch provides a good approach to Plateau and makes an enjoyable hike. Stony Clove provides a shorter trip to Plateau's top ridge, has a State-run campground, and provides a perspective of the Devil's Path unavailable from the east, plus Stony Clove's striking depths and lush forest make this overture worth climbing the additional 250 feet of elevation.

The approach from Stony Clove is steep. Plateau's ice-scoured slopes hold a veneer of glacial till abandoned by the Wisconsin Ice Sheet. The Catskills' typical northern hardwood forest is absent. A mixed hardwood forest coats the mountainside. Diamond-patterned white ash and smooth, silvery-gray American beech dominate the forest. Bigtooth aspen and black cherry are also common. An early successional species, bigtooth aspen attest to open slopes at the time they sprouted. The aspen's age is the forest's age.

Other evidence supports this observation. The biggest trees are all about the same size. In ideal conditions, most trees that fill similar niches grow at similar rates, so size can roughly relate to age on sites with uniform conditions. Here, the largest white ash are similar in diameter to the largest bigtooth aspen. Both species require plentiful sunlight, and no saplings of either species are present.

The second-growth forest is ripe with change. Beech and striped maple grow beneath the canopy. When young, the shade-tolerant species grow slower in sunlight than pioneer species. After the forest matures and the pioneers die, the beech will dominate. This strategy earns the beech a place in the canopy.

North of the trail, still near the clove's bottom, a large rock slide lies frozen on the mountainside. As it occurred recently, no vegetation or soil gathers among the broken sandstone slope. A distinctive landmark, this slide is but one of many cascading Plateau's slopes. Rock slides occur on steep, unstable slopes. Rearranged by erosion and glaciation, unstable slopes are common throughout the Catskills. Rain and mud provide the lubrication for movement.

The trail steepens after passing the rock slide. The forest remains a mix of pioneers and shade-tolerant species. A stream parallels the trail's southern flank, nestled in a steep ravine. At the trail's lowest switchback, the stream's gentle cascade increases to a roar as a small series of waterfalls leap over sandstone steps. The falls, lively in the spring or after a storm, nestle among a cozy valley. Moss lines the streambed, creating a soft, green waterway. The trail, however, ignores this waterfall and continues its winding, upward route. The stream's busy waters fade to background noise, leaving only bird calls and the wind to stir the air.

As the trail leaves the deep valley, Hunter Mountain appears across Stony Clove, its massive slopes a constant companion. When on Plateau's lower slopes, the highest visible part of Hunter, a 3,100-foot ridge, provides a benchmark for measuring progress. Stony Clove sits at 1,950 feet. Hunter's low ridge lifts 1,150 feet above it. A parallel sighting across the clove provides a reliable estimate of elevation. Higher on Plateau, Hunter's 4,040-foot summit dwarfs this ridge, its silver fire tower piercing the sky. Remember to use caution when identifying Hunter's ridges, since they have similar outlines.

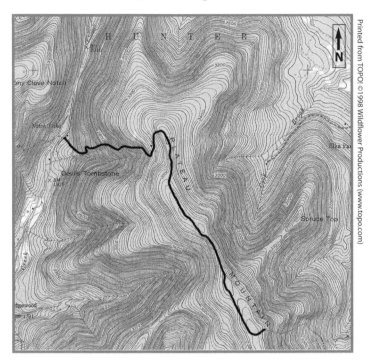

Tree heights shrink with increasing elevation, revealing peaks of varying distances. A high ridge that merges with Plateau's long summit fills the northern sky. To the south a lone peak, 4,180-foot Slide Mountain, rises above the surrounding terrain. Open slopes created by landslides provide additional glimpses of Slide and other nearby peaks.

Forest composition changes as elevation increases. The higher slopes provide an environment with cooler temperatures, higher precipitation, and thinner soils. Yellow and paper birch replace the beech, bigtooth aspen, and white ash. Thin, rocky soils and landslides limit tree cover, and the slides are often devoid of trees. Many of the birch are first generation. Sprouting through the rock fields without competition for light, these trees can spread horizontally, their ball-shaped crowns maximizing sunlight and minimizing wind exposure.

Stone characterizes the climb on Plateau. Rocks coat the mountainside and litter the trail. The rock slides are sterile sandstone avenues. The stones, a constant theme, suggest the idea of renaming Plateau Mountain as "Stony Mountain." Today's adventurers are not the first to make this observation. Arnold Henry Guyot, during his quest to map and measure the Catskills in the late 1870s, named this mountain "Stony Mountain." Plateau persevered though, and remains the official name.

The trail levels before reaching the top ridge. It moves through an upper hardwood forest while a small stream meanders alongside the path. Aided by gravity, the water makes a quicker descent than the trail. Soon these waters will tumble down the moss-covered falls in the clove.

After parting with the stream, the trail traverses soggy ground. The dark soils, rich in organic matter, are shallow and often saturated with water. Overall, growing conditions are poor. Small, stubby trees, widely-spaced shrubs, and thick, matted grasses cover the land. Red spruce grow on the coolest, most sheltered sites, attesting to the boreal conditions. Coarse, gray rock outcrops appear as the trail approaches the 3,500-foot line. The cross-bedded sandstones are river deposits from the Devonian Period. The Appalachian Orogeny, 225 million years ago, thrust these rocks into part of a great plateau. Erosion carved this plateau into the Catskill Mountains. Ice ages rounded and polished exposed rock. After the ice sheets retreated, glacial tills covered the lower elevations, but on the Catskills' mountaintops the bedrock often shows through the till.

After twisting up Plateau's chaotic western slopes, the trail reaches the long, flat summit. At Orchard Ledge, its northwestern terminus, a 180-degree panorama centers on the southwest. Saturated with the sweet scent of balsam wafted by cool breezes, the wide, flat ledge provides excellent viewing and napping opportunities. A forest of red spruce, mountain-ash, yellow birch, and paper birch fence the ledge.

The view is spectacular. Hunter Mountain sits across the depths of Stony Clove. It rises 440 feet above this ledge and dominates the western skyline. North of Hunter, Onteora Mountain and the East Jewett Range lift from the Schoharie Valley. To the northwest, Cave Mountain,

Looking northeast toward Kaaterskill High Peak and Roundtop

home to Ski Windham, anchors the view. Belleayre Mountain's ski trails stand out south of Hunter. In early spring, icy stripes clearly identify the ski slopes. Southeast of Belleayre is Balsam Mountain, followed by Haynes and Eagle Mountains. Graham Mountain's massive shape engulfs Eagle. West of Graham, the land rises to crest as Balsam Lake Mountain. East of Belleayre is the Panther Mountain Circle. Its northeastern quarter is Garfield Mountain. Panther leads south to Giant Ledge and then Slide Mountain. East of Slide is Table Mountain. The ridgeline then heads northeast capping Friday, Cornell, and Wittenberg Mountains. Ashokan High Point and Samuels Point lie east of this high ridge. Mount Tremper, its flat top distinctive among the lower peaks, merges with smaller hills and ridges lining Chichester Creek.

The trail follows the main ridge southeast. After a short distance, an open cliff top provides an impressive northerly view. The East Jewett Range and Onteora Mountain lie northwest. Windham High Peak and the Blackhead mountains dominate the northern skyline.

Kaaterskill High Peak, Roundtop, and Clum Hill rise northeast across the Schoharie Valley, easily recognized by their distinctive shapes.

The two-mile ridge follows Plateau's namesake to the summit. Orchard Ledge is 240 feet below the true summit at the ridge's eastern end. The forest covering Plateau's main ridge is typical of the Catskills. Dense thickets of young red spruce and balsam fir dominate the community, while an occasional paper birch or hobblebush peppers the landscape. A thick carpet of bronze needles coats the rich, dark soil. The decaying needles and dark humus hold most of the forest's nutrients.

Plateau's highest point passes unannounced by man or nature. The slight slope simply levels and starts for Mink Hollow. The thick, spruce-fir forest constricts the trail as it starts the 1,400-foot descent. Along the way, a small, exposed outcrop provides an open view southeast. Overlook Mountain leaps from the Hudson Valley, the keen eye finding its 300-foot television tower splitting the sky. Overlook's outline leads toward the vast Ashokan Reservoir and the smaller Cooper Lake. Sugarloaf Mountain dominates the foreground, its massive form contrasting with wispy clouds and ethereal sky. Once below the vista, a northern hardwood forest escorts the path to Mink Hollow.

Although the Devil's Path continues west of Plateau, Route 214 effectively isolates this range. Thus permanently scarred by man, the mountain wilderness ends at the highway. The Devil's Path's other mountains provide separate adventures. The elements linking Indian Head, Twin, Sugarloaf, and Plateau do not easily extend to Hunter and Westkill.

So ends the trek along the Devil's Path. It is a mix of challenge and reward. Steep mountainsides test determination and stamina, while majestic views and accomplishment await those completing the challenge. The Devil's Path, a place of harsh beauty and grandeur, remains one of the Catskills' wildest places, a last refuge from civilization's influence.

HUNTER

Hike: Hunter
Roundtrip Hiking Distance: 4.4 miles
County and Town: Greene, Hunter
Parking: Route 214, State parking area 1 mile south of Route 214/23A
intersection (small pull-off on west side of road for Becker Hollow
Trail)
Difficulty: difficult
Bushwhack: no
Elevation Gain: 2200 feet
Mile: 0.0: Begin Becker Hollow Trail along NY Route 214
0.4: Pass concrete dam
2.0: Reach summit ridge, trail ends. Turn north (right)
2.2: Summit clearing, fire tower. Return via same route
2.4: Return to top of Becker Hollow; turn left
4.4: Return to parking area

Hunter Mountain is the Catskills' second highest peak. Only Slide
Mountain, 15 miles to the south, lifts higher than Hunter's 4,040-foot
summit. Although not first in elevation, Hunter's accessible location
and popular ski center make it the Catskills' best-known peak. Named
for Edward Hunter, a 19th-century leather tanner, the mountain
encompasses three distinct peaks. In the nearby Village of Hunter,
workers tanned more than 2.2 million hides. Timber companies and
lumberjacks cut the region's massive hemlock forests to provide tannic
acid for the process.

Hunter Mountain is part of the northern Catskills, and is the tra-
ditional western terminus of the Devil's Path Mountains (the trail actually continues on to Westkill Mountain). Stony Clove borders Hunter's
steep eastern flank. The sharp pass is the lowest notch connecting the
Schoharie and Esopus Valleys. New York Route 214 occupies the pass,
slicing Hunter from its companions. Also nestled in the clove is a small,

picturesque lake and a State-run campsite, Devil's Tombstone. The Devil's Path Trail climbs Hunter's eastern face, but it is not the only way to ascend Hunter. Ranging from easy to difficult, Hunter's foot trails mimic the mountain's north-facing ski trails.

The Becker Hollow Trail is the shortest route to the summit. It is a steep, challenging hike. The trail begins north of Stony Clove, off Route 214, at an elevation of 1,820 feet. After two miles of stiff climbing, it merges with a wider trail atop the 4,000-foot-high ridge holding the peak. The wide path heads north from the summit to the 80-foot fire tower.

From the small parking area, a well-worn trail leads into an old field. Flowers spread color throughout the sunny glade from April until October. Purple spring beauties and yellow, white, and common violets begin the annual parade, their gentle perfumes freshening the spring air. Summer greenery sets the stage for Canada thistle, New York asters, fire pinks, and goldenrod. Grasshoppers and katydids hum in July's heat.

A young generation of trees shade part of the evolving field, the forest working to reclaim this ground through succession. In time, the trees will shade and then kill the sun-loving plants. Filled mainly with pioneer tree species, the field supports a healthy set of white pine, red maple, black birch, yellow birch, and paper birch. Even some late successional species—beech, hemlock, and sugar maple—live in the field. The same species grow in the nearby forests, but the open conditions here allow them to spread into full, bushy forms.

The trail maintains an easy grade as it follows a stream from the open field to a wooded area. Despite Mother Nature's reclamation efforts, signs of human habitation are apparent. An old roadbed parallels the trail. Once it led to a farmstead; now it struggles to maintain a presence. Retaining walls, built to contain the stream when bloated with spring meltwater, line the watercourse. Filled with rock and debris from a thousand storms, these aging structures face obliteration. Water pipes —some dull aluminum, others coated with rust—follow the trail. Broken in many places, this defunct system functions only as a reminder of yesterday's uses.

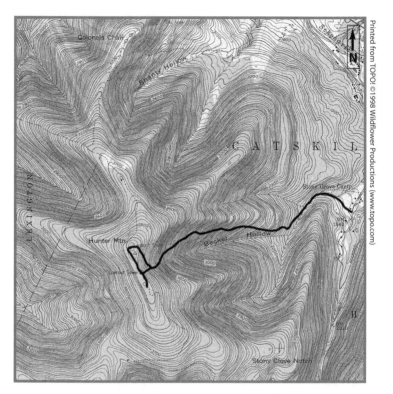

With the trail moving deeper into the forest, the trees become larger and older. Forest composition remains unchanged, a collection of maple, pine, beech, and birch. The dense canopy shades the ground, leaving it cool, dark, and barren. Shade-tolerant understory plants still need time to establish themselves. Thin trunks and dense populations confirm this forest's youthful character. Crowded by neighbors, the thin trees reach for light. To fall into shade means death. Neighboring trees quickly colonize any open gaps.

The lowlands along the stream and Becker Hollow Trail support third-growth forests. Massive hemlock trees once dominated these lowland areas, but were cut for the nearby leather tanneries. Despite poor logging practices and fires, the forests returned. In the late 1800s, the second-growth forest provided wood for fuel and a booming barrel hoop industry.

The stream and trail remain together, both beginning a gentle ascent. The stream's light current becomes a playful babble. Roadbeds and side trails lead into the forest. No longer able to share the shrinking valley, the stream and trail divorce. Within a few hundred feet, the path rises sharply. Slope increases, and within a few steps the trail becomes very steep. It holds this ascent for the next two miles. Scrambles over rock ledges and hand-over-hand climbing are not necessary, but it is still a tiring journey that taxes the hardiest of hikers. Despite the trail's incline, it has many attractive features, including a direct approach to Hunter's summit. The land it traverses is quiet and wild. Many animals inhabit this rugged, isolated area. Ruffed grouse, porcupines, squirrels, skunks, and bear thrive here.

The ascent up Becker Hollow follows one of Hunter's steepest shoulders. Another shoulder lifts south of Becker Hollow and remains in sight for the entire journey. Plateau Mountain rises as Stony Clove's eastern wall. These nearby landforms make it easy to estimate elevation. A horizontal sighting at eye level of Plateau gives a reading with reference to its 3,840-foot summit and 2,000-foot lower slopes. With a topographic map, it is easy to determine the lowest elevation visible on Plateau. The relative vertical distance between the estimate, the summit, and lowest visible point gives a reliable measurement of elevation.

After two miles, the invigorating climb ends. Near the incline's end, the northern hardwood forest gives way to red spruce and balsam fir. First, the forest types combine, but the transition is quick. Soon the subalpine forest stands alone to brave the cool, windy conditions. On average, the temperature drops 11F degrees between the parking area and Hunter's summit. Once the slope moderates, it is an easy walk to the main ridge.

A large collection of human and animal trails crisscross Hunter's main ridge. West of the Becker Hollow Trail junction, an open sandstone ledge provides an excellent lookout south and west. Typical of Catskill summits, this uncovered, horizontal sandstone block provides

The eastern view from the tower reveals Kaaterskill High Peak and Roundtop

a comfortable and beautiful rest stop. The unobstructed ledge offers one of the northern Catskills' best views. A quarter mile away, Southwest Hunter's domed peak dominates the foreground. Westkill Mountain (3,880 feet) lifts beyond Southwest Hunter. Rusk Mountain (3,680 feet) fills the northwestern horizon. West of Rusk runs the ridge supporting Evergreen and Pine Mountains. Between Rusk and Westkill, Hunter's western slopes enclose Spruceton Valley. The steep mountain walls resulted from large-scale glacial scouring. Slide Mountain silently looms to the south, overshadowing its neighbors. East of Slide is the rest of the Burroughs Range: Wittenberg, Cornell, Friday, and Balsam Cap Mountains.

The summit and fire tower lie north. The path is like a wide boulevard leading to an important, but rarely visited, destination. Lined by thousands of spruce and fir trees, the trail funnels into a large clearing, with the fire tower standing at the center. Dense vegetation blocks the view, leaving the tower as the only option for vista seekers. This structure is solid, unlike many of the Catskills' fire towers. After climbing a few flights, the surrounding terrain spreads in a wide circle. Once above the trees, the wind increases, chilling tired hikers and shaking the tower.

The view encompasses most of the Catskills. To the south rise the central high peaks. To the east is the rest of the Devil's Path. Northwestern Catskill peaks, including Westkill, Rusk, Northdome, Sherill, Vly, and Bearpen, create a spectacular backdrop for sunsets. The northwest holds the glacially-beaten East Jewett Range and the Schoharie Valley. In the northeast, the Blackhead Range lifts above a foreground of Onteora Mountain. Parker Hill is south of the Blackheads, along with the duo of Kaaterskill High Peak and Roundtop. When looking at their western faces, this pair has a unique perspective, and their distinctive silhouette changes almost beyond recognition.

Despite its incredible views, people best know Hunter for its skiing. The ski center's upper slopes stand out to the northwest. Colonel's Chair, a noteworthy lookout 1,000 feet below, caps the ski area. A trail to Colonel's Chair begins at the summit, and the ski area's chair lifts also provide access.

As one of two Catskill points above 4,000 feet, and the second highest summit between the Adirondacks and Shenandoah National Park in Virginia, Hunter Mountain has few equals. Its wildlife, challenging hikes, awe-inspiring ledges, and 360-degree panorama make it a worthy exploration opportunity.

THE NORTHERN CATSKILLS

Overrun by a series of continental ice sheets, the northern Catskills reflect their glacial heritage. Rounded and smooth, the mountains are simple. Few side ridges and shoulders complicate the topography. Most of the gentle summits, especially those along the Batavia Kill Valley, lost their higher elevations to the glaciers, yet some of the Catskills' highest peaks, the Blackheads, loom along its northern front. At the Catskills' northeastern corner sits Windham High Peak.

Looking south at the Blackhead Range

THE BLACKHEAD RANGE

Hike: Blackheads (Thomas Cole, Black Dome, Blackhead)
One-way Hiking Distance: 6.1 miles
County and Town: Greene, Jewett
Parking: Eastern end of Barnum Road, (off Maplecrest Road—County Route 40), and eastern end of Big Hollow Road (eastern terminus of Black Dome Valley)
Difficulty: difficult
Bushwhack: no
Elevation Gain: 1800 feet
(one-way hike; requires two vehicles)
Mile: 0.0: Start from parking area on Barnum Road (off County Road 40) (red markers)
 0.4: Trail bends from southeast to northeast and enters state land
 0.9: Viewpoint south located at a switchback
 1.5: Summit of Camel's Hump
 2.4: Summit of Thomas Cole
 3.2: Summit of Black Dome
 3.6: Go straight, following the Blackhead Mountain Trail (yellow markers)
 4.1: Summit of Blackhead, turn northeast on to escarpment trail (blue markers)
 4.8: Turn west (left) at junction with Batavia Kill Trail (yellow markers)
 6.1: Reach parking area at end of Black Dome Valley Road

Each morning, the sun's first rays sprint over the Hudson River to strike the Catskills' eastern escarpment. The imposing mountain wall parallels the upper Mid-Hudson Valley and separates mountain from lowland. Only two streams, Kaaterskill and Plattekill Creeks, breach this barrier. North of these tumbling watercourses, the escarpment runs uninterrupted to Windham High Peak. In this space lifts Blackhead Mountain's 3,940-foot summit, the escarpment's highest point. Behind Blackhead rise its brother mountains: 3,990-foot Black

Dome and 3,940-foot Thomas Cole. These three mountains, the Blackhead Range, are the Catskills' third, fourth, and fifth highest summits. All three peaks hold adventure, incredible views, and a fascinating natural history.

The Blackhead Range's northern slopes fall into Black Dome Valley. The Batavia Kill, a tributary of Schoharie Creek, flows westward along the sheltered vale's floor. The valley is much wider than the Batavia Kill. When the mile-high continental ice sheets invaded this isolated basin, they eroded, expanded, and reworked the area into a wide U-shaped valley. When the Wisconsin Ice Sheet retreated 11,000 years ago, it deposited unsorted debris over the landscape. The till sediments range in size from sand grains to boulders, and include 100 feet or more of material. Till depths decrease with elevation, and many mountaintops and high ridges remain free of these glacial sediments.

A radial drainage pattern characterizes the Blackheads. The Batavia Kill's headwater streams collect runoff from the Blackhead's northern slopes and join with waters from Windham's southern face. After moving west for 20 miles, the Batavia Kill merges into Schoharie Creek. Waters from the Blackhead's southern slopes flow into East Kill Creek. It also flows west, reaching the Schoharie 12 miles upstream of the Batavia Kill. Blackhead Mountain's eastern slopes drain into the Shingle Kill, a small tributary of Catskill Creek.

An east-west trail provides access to the Blackheads. Dayhikes that include the three peaks work best when leaving a vehicle at each end. Situated 1,100 feet higher, the western trailhead has an easier initial climb. When approached from the west, Thomas Cole is the first challenge, its summit looming 1,840 feet above the parking area.

As with many Catskill trails, the western approach begins as an old logging road. The path moves through young forests, old clearings, and gentle slopes. The mixed hardwood forest, an assortment of northern red oak, chestnut oak, sugar maple, and beech, line the sun-baked, red clay trail. Quaking aspen and an occasional white pine dominate the

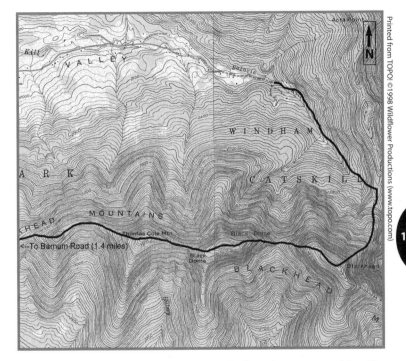

Printed from TOPO! ©1998 Wildflower Productions (www.topo.com)

old clearings. Aspen have orange-green bark and are easy to identify. The aspen leaves dance in the wind.

Pioneer species fill the sun-bathed clearings. Grasses, flowers, herbs, and trees weave a dense green mat over the earth. Most Catskill fields result from past logging and farming activities, but natural phenomena such as lightning, fires, and windstorms also create open areas. The forest reclaims these fields through the process of succession. Pioneer trees, including pines and aspens, are first to establish in cleared areas. Plentiful sunlight, dry soils, and a lack of competition help these species thrive. Within a few decades the pioneer species shade the field, killing ground-level vegetation.

Aspen cannot grow in shade. Their light, wind-blown seeds must find a new, unshaded location. Aspens are so dependent on direct sunlight that they self-prune shaded branches. Pines also thrive in the open areas. As these species mature, they shade the ground and change the environment. Shade-tolerant species sprout beneath the canopy. Oaks, able to grow in patchy shade, often replace pioneer species. Northern red and chestnut oak are the Catskills' most common oaks. They do best in slightly xeric (dry), lightly-shaded habitats, especially on western and southern faces. Mature oaks often reach heights of 120 feet. Aggressive light-seekers, the oaks' sprawling limbs quickly fill any canopy gaps. Once established, the oaks' canopy provides heavy shade. This conserves soil moisture and reduces forest floor temperatures. Often the cooler, darker, and moister habitat cannot support oak seedlings, and they yield to the Catskills' climax forest of northern hardwoods. Maples, especially shade-tolerant sugar maple, thrive. Able to grow in deep shade, they can dominate forest stands for generations. American beech also prosper in shade. They can survive 80 years without direct sunlight. Both species wait for a small canopy gap. When one opens, they spurt into the opening to join the canopy. Once mature, all trees need strong sunlight, but many seedlings and saplings of shade-tolerant species wilt and die under the sun's direct rays. These different growing strategies reduce competition between species.

After a gentle climb along the wide, State-marked path, a sign-in box marks a change in the land's character. Slopes increase, and the forest is older. Spring flowers color the route. Violets, foamflower, painted trillium, kidney-leaf buttercup, and scores of purple trillium line the trail's sunny edges. The route continues its sharp rise, rapidly lifting the trail above the adjoining valleys. A switchback places the trail atop a small sandstone overhang and introduces a pleasant scene. An excellent view opens to the southwest. Across the Schoharie Valley rise Hunter and Plateau Mountains. Stony Clove separates the two peaks. Beyond the deep clove is the Burroughs Range. West of Hunter, Westkill's sharp peak slices into the blue sky.

The taxing climb continues until the trail tops a 3,300-foot peak. The higher elevations bring a decrease in tree height and changes in composition. Yellow birch and black cherry become the most common forest community members. After crossing the small, unnamed peak,

A northeastern view from Blackhead Mountain overlooks the escarpment and Acra Point

the trail dips before slowly rising again, and leads to 3,500-foot Camel's Hump. Covered with raspberries, blackberries, and hobblebush, the scruffy-looking ridgetop produces a bountiful fall harvest. Beyond Camel's Hump, the trail settles into a small notch, and then turns southeast to face Thomas Cole's imposing mass. The 400-foot climb is relentlessly strenuous.

Thomas Cole Mountain takes its name from the famous painter, founder of the Hudson River School of landscape art. Known for its lifelike scenery in the pre-photography era, the movement specialized in the vast, unspoiled American landscape. Among Cole's best-known works are scenes of Kaaterskill Falls, the Catskill Mountain House, and views along the escarpment wall. Before its renaming as Thomas Cole, the explorer Arnold Henry Guyot named this peak Mount Kimball, after one of his assistants. Locals often referred to it as Black Tom.

The northern hardwood forest yields the mountain slopes to a sub-alpine community as elevation tops 3,500 feet. The vegetation and the weather reflect the boreal conditions. Balsam fir cover the mountain, accompanied by a few stands of red spruce. Soft, dark foliage and the balsam's sweet aroma blanket the dome-shaped mountain. The cool, damp conditions support some of the Catskills' thickest, healthiest fir stands. The summit is often 20F degrees cooler than the Hudson Valley, and it receives 65 inches of annual precipitation. Up to 200 inches of snow can fall in a year.

Thomas Cole's only view opens to the south. A spur trail south leads to a small ledge. Limited by encroaching vegetation, the once tremendous view is only a shadow of its former beauty. Well below the trail, on the mountain's southwestern face, a series of impressive over-looks top small rock overhangs. Views peer upon neighboring Black Dome and Blackhead Mountains. Other views span the western horizon, including peaks as far away as Bearpen, Utsayantha and Balsam Lake Mountains.

After the viewpoint, the path crosses the mountaintop and descends into a notch. The drop ends quickly. The lowest ground between Thomas Cole and Black Dome Mountains is 3,730 feet. Technically, this notch is not deep enough to consider the two mountains separate. Sheltered by the nearby peaks, a stout northern hardwood forest of sugar maple, beech, and birch thrives here. Sugar maple rarely survives at these elevations and is usually absent from forest stands by 3,300 feet. From the notch, a look east previews the 260-foot climb to the Catskills' third highest summit, Black Dome Mountain.

For a few years in the mid-1800s, Black Dome Mountain gained acceptance as the Catskills' highest peak. Maps from the period labeled the mountain as Blacktop. Although many people believed Black Dome was higher than Kaaterskill High Peak, local resort owners in the Kaaterskill Region denied this claim. Despite 300 additional feet of rock, and accurate measurements, the truth remained muddled for years. Owners wanted guests to believe that the Catskills' highest peak stood right by their hotels. Black Dome's official recognition as the

Catskills' highest peak ended quickly as measurements established Hunter Mountain as higher than Black Dome.

Black Dome's rounded summit resembles Thomas Cole's. A dark mantle of balsam fir and a few red spruce clothe the mountaintop. Although precipitation is plentiful, the thin soil holds little moisture. Dried grasses and wilted plants invade open areas.

The sandstone ledge capping the summit has a limited view south, as paper birch and balsam fir trees obscure the scene. As the trail continues east, it opens onto a spectacular vista 100 feet below the summit. The view is among the Catskills' most striking. Perched atop a small cliff, the exposed ledge blossoms into a 180-degree panorama. From Hunter Mountain in the southwest, the view wraps counterclockwise to Windham High Peak. A southern exposure helps dispel the chill air. Blackhead Mountain dominates the eastern sky. To the south, in East Kill's Valley, Colgate and Capra Lakes sparkle in the sunlight. Rising on the small valley's far side are Stoppel Point and North Mountain. Kaaterskill High Peak and Roundtop rise on the next ridge. The Devil's Path Mountains form a massive wall on the Schoharie's south side. The Catskills' central high peaks show through its deep notches. Overlook Mountain anchors the escarpment wall's southeastern limit.

After the vista, the trail slips between Black Dome and Blackhead Mountains. The descent is easy. The higher summits protect these slopes from the cold, strong winds, and create habitat for sugar maple, striped maple, and beech. Other species in the sheltered gap include yellow birch, paper birch, and black cherry. The local trees are taller and have better form. A blanket of quiet coats the nearby forest, projecting a sense of calm through the col. But first steps along the steep 500-foot climb to Blackhead Mountain break the notch's peaceful spell.

Purple trillium abound throughout the Blackheads, especially in the sheltered notches. Members of the lily family, the indigo-colored flowers have three petals, three sepals, and three leaves. Unlike most flowers, purple trillium depend on flies for pollination. To attract the flies, they produce a nectar that smells of rotting meat.

Once above 3,800 feet, eroded sand and sandstones litter the path reducing traction, and forest cover decreases. A 270-degree vista opens with Blackhead Mountain's summit blocking the eastern view. The southern view offers a slightly different perspective of the view from Black Dome Mountain. Black Dome dominates the western skyline, and Thomas Cole peeks from behind it.

The Blackhead's distinctive shapes are unique among the Catskills. Each appears as an overturned bowl rising above their shared ridge. No side ridges protrude from the domed mountaintops. Clues to these atypical Catskill shapes relate to the local geology. The exposed rocks forming the Blackhead Range are among the Catskills' oldest. The entire ridge shows evidence of uplift. Tectonic forces may have vaulted this range above its neighbors, perhaps a few thousand feet above the surrounding rock strata. The lifted lands became the Catskills' highest peaks. Since that time, water, wind, and ice worked to erode the protruding landscape. With additional potential energy, erosion rates are faster on higher ground. Today, the three peaks display only a fraction of their former height.

The Blackhead's bedrock is uncommon among the Catskill peaks. Thin strata characterize the local sandstones, contrasting with the thick, blocky layers of other nearby summits. Well sorted, the similar-sized grains cement poorly. The Catskills evolved from sands and silts transported from the east. The Blackhead's sands were Devonian Era beachfront property until buried by expanding river deltas. The local uplift, occurring recently in geologic time, thrust the beach sands above the river delta sediments.

Conifers cover Blackhead Mountain. It has no summit views, but a short bushwhack southwest leads to a small, exposed rock outcrop. The pleasant view opens southward. Blackhead holds the distinction of being the Catskills' tallest mountain, possessing the most relief from its 1,000-foot lowest slopes to its 3,940-foot summit.

From Blackhead's summit, two trails head onto the escarpment wall. The northern route heads toward Acra Point and Black Dome Valley. The southern fork leads to North Mountain. The descent into

Black Dome Valley is long and steep. Knees and ankles often protest this difficult journey. A few views peer over the escarpment wall to the Hudson Valley and Cairo Round Top. Small overlooks northeast reveal Acra Point and Burnt Knob.

Conditions warm as elevation decreases. Deeper soils and milder climate help the forest grow thicker and taller. Glimpses of Blackhead's summit slip through the tall trees. From this perspective, its towering mass is a mountain skyscraper. Few Catskill locations reveal this much relief. The trail then leads northwest into Black Dome Valley. A spring and lean-to nestle along the trail as it reaches the valley floor.

This triple mountain hike is a challenging trek for the body. The peaks' distinctive geology and geography distinguish the area in the mind. The three plain domes overlook hundreds of beautiful square miles. Although an integral part of the Catskills, the Blackheads create an atmosphere all their own.

Spruce-fir forest covers the Blackhead's summit

WINDHAM HIGH PEAK

Hike: Windham High Peak
Roundtrip Hiking Distance: 7.6 miles
County and Town: Greene, Windham
Parking: Near eastern end of Big Hollow Road, trail on north side of road
Difficulty: moderate-difficult
Bushwhack: no
Elevation Gain: 1300 feet
Mile: 0.0: Trail (red markers) begins at parking area on Big Hollow Road; head north
   1.1: Trail ends at Escarpment Trail (blue markers); Turn west (left)
   2.4: Trail reaches highest point along Burnt Knob
   3.0: Notch between Burnt Knob and Windham
   3.8: Summit of Windham. Views from both sides of the summit. Return via same route
   6.5: Turn south back into Black Dome Valley
   7.6: Return to parking area on Big Hollow Road

Windham High Peak marks the Catskills' northeastern cornerstone. For 100 miles, the Catskills' northern front marches northwest from this imposing anchor. South and west of Windham, the Catskills rise in a series of ridges, peaks, and isolated valleys. Directly south of Windham, across Black Dome Valley, rise the Blackhead Range's giant sandstone domes.

Small streams and their basins encircle Windham High Peak from northwest to south. In the distance, the tame Hudson and Mohawk river valleys lap against the Catskills' forests. To the east, the Hudson River flows like a decorative blue ribbon through lush, green fields. A tidal river, the sea-level Hudson slowly melds with the ocean. In the seven miles between the river and the Catskills' escarpment, the land lifts 700 feet. The next mile brings the land to Windham High Peak's

3,524-foot summit. From Albany, 40 miles to the north, Windham soars into the southern horizon.

Approaches to Windham lead from the east, south, and west. The eastern path, which follows the escarpment, also skirts Burnt Knob, providing a scenic journey. This path passes through second-growth forest as it climbs Black Dome Valley's northeastern face. After crossing a small stream, the trail ascends the escarpment's backside. Copper conifer needles carpet the path, the soft ground cover muffling footsteps and voices, providing quiet moments to observe the local fauna. Wild turkey, deer, and bear frequent the area. The path gets steeper as it climbs. From scattered vantages, the forest profile parts enough to reveal the U-shaped Black Dome Valley.

Heavily scoured during the last ice age, this isolated valley formed when huge ice flows plowed into it from the west. When the ice retreated, it left a thick till layer. Deepest on the valley floor—up to 100 feet in places—till depths decrease as elevation increases. Beneath the till, horizontal sandstone and shale layers support the Catskill Mountains and give them a stair-step appearance. The glacial sediments burying the area's lower slopes smooth the topography. Most areas above 3,300 feet hold only a few inches of till, so exposed sandstone ledges in the higher elevations protrude from the veneer. As a result, the Catskills' upper elevations retain the bedrock's stair-step topography.

The northern spur of the Black Dome Range trail is a direct route to the escarpment wall, passing through a forest of even-aged sugar maple and beech. Hemlocks line the cool streambanks. Non-native conifers, mainly Norway spruce planted during reforestation projects, thrive along the lower slopes, a replacement for the hemlock stands. The sunny slopes allow sun-loving pioneers to thrive in the aftermath of heavy logging and grazing. Black cherry, easily identified by its dark, potato chip bark, grows well. Northern red oak, uncommon in the Catskills west of the escarpment, dominates drier sites. White ash and big toothed aspen, pioneer species, are also common.

The sun-loving species attest to once-open ground. The age of these trees, about 80 years, is the forest's age. Aspens can only grow in

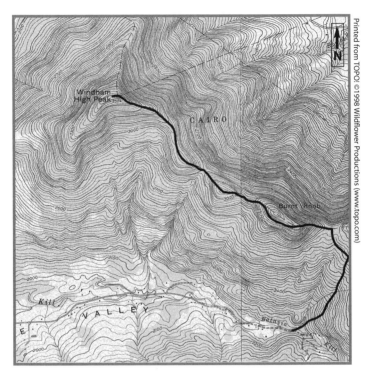

Printed from TOPO! © 1998 Wildflower Productions (www.topo.com)

direct sunlight, and ash require sunny conditions, further attesting to a past clearing. Other signs provide additional evidence of the area's landscape history: there are no mature trees, and the largest are about the same size which means they began to grow at about the same time. If undisturbed for a few centuries, shade-tolerant species will return to dominate the mountainside. Mature and over-mature trees will dominate an old-growth forest. Only in gaps will sun-loving trees survive. Black cherry is the most common gap species.

The trail ends after completing the surprisingly easy climb up the escarpment's backside. From the trail junction, the escarpment trail heads west to Burnt Knob and Windham High Peak. Abrupt ecological changes accompany the turn onto the escarpment ridge. Northern red oak is now the most common species. They rarely survive above 2,500 feet, as the cool, damp conditions limit growth and reproduction. Along the escarpment, dry, exposed slopes, past fires, and a proximity to the Hudson Valley's milder climate allow oaks to survive to 3,300 feet.

After reaching the escarpment trail, the slope increases to rival the Catskills' steepest trails. The sharp climb ends at a series of east and south-facing ledges. The open views are an excellent excuse to stop and rest straining lungs and muscles. Northern red oaks frame the ledge, while northern hardwoods blanket Black Dome Valley. The oak border also frames an eastern vista filled by Acra Point, the escarpment wall, and the Hudson Valley. The low, rounded, and ancient hills composing the Taconics and Berkshires rise east of the Hudson Valley. Mount Everett, near the Connecticut-Massachusetts border, is the most conspicuous of these gentle forms.

The Blackheads dominate the southern view, their eastern peak anchored by the 3,940-foot Blackhead Mountain. In the center stands 3,990-foot Black Dome, and 3,940-foot Thomas Cole marks the western summit. A curious and isolated set of mountains, these peaks are the Catskills' third, fourth, and fifth highest points. Rich in diversity and scientific mystery, this ridge has some unique geologic characteristics.

Black Dome Valley's U-shape is well illustrated from this platform. Glaciers smoothed landscapes, and when the ice sheets retreated, the Catskills emerged with their rounded, subdued slopes. The ice sheets' erosional power also redefined local and regional drainage patterns. As water drained from the newly emerged slopes, it formed new V-shaped valleys. Many small stream valleys carve the mountain slopes. Created from smooth landscapes, these small drainages represent 10,000 years of water erosion.

Using those 10,000 years as a reference, the progression of stream erosion unfolds. A look across the valley reveals a few of these young drainages. Imagine them 10,000 years into the future, twice as wide and deep. Then imagine them 100,000 years into the future, ten times deeper and wider. Sharp ravines, rounded ridges, and small gorges will dominate the landscape. Expanded stream valleys will reach farther

A side trip to Acra Point provides a great view of Burnt Knob and Windham High Peak

upslope. Erosion will continue, and in a million years these small stream valleys will be 100 times bigger. Deep gorges will separate carved ridges. Roaring waterfalls will form on resistant rock layers. Intricate drainage patterns will sculpt the landscape like the Grand Canyon. When taken in steps, the reduction of a mountain range to a rolling plain is easier to comprehend. A projection of only a million years into the Catskills' future reveals profound changes. Imagine 10 million or 50 million years into the future: entire mountain ranges can erode and disappear. Conditions rarely remain constant for a million years, however, so a landscape's future always remains uncertain. Ice sheets may return, lowering and rounding the landscape again and erasing current drainage patterns. After these ice sheets retreat, the process begins again.

The trail then crosses Burnt Knob's southern face and passes a series of southwest-facing lookouts. They peer across the Schoharie Valley to a low ridge and the northern Catskills' higher peaks. Thomas

Cole's western shoulder and Camel's Hump hold the eastern foreground. Westkill, the Catskills' sixth highest peak, juts into the southwestern sky. Rusk Mountain blocks most of Westkill, and is the highest point along the ridge it shares with Evergreen, Packsaddle, and Pine Island Mountains.

The East Jewett Range, partially hidden by Thomas Cole, eclipses Rusk's lower slopes. Van Loan Hill and Round Hill rise west of the East Jewett Range. West of Pine Island are Halcott, Vly, and Bearpen Mountains, parallelling the Schoharie Valley as it bends northward. Cave and Tower Mountains compose the western foreground. Ski Windham's slopes identify Cave Mountain. Bearpen's higher slopes rise above these low mountains. Roundtop Mountain lies north of Bearpen, its outline partially eclipsed by Windham's imposing shoulder.

The trail remains level as it skirts the ridge's southwestern face. Small stems of paper birch, yellow birch, northern red oak, beech, sugar maple, and black cherry compose the forest. Like most of the northern Catskills, this second growth replaces ancient forests logged in the 1800s.

After descending a steep rock face, the trail migrates to the ridge's north face. An open cliff provides a spectacular view of Windham High Peak and the lowlands to its north and northwest. On a clear day, the Adirondacks and Green Mountains stand out along the northern and northeastern horizons. Autumn paints fiery islands of color on this emerald green canvas. Spectacular fall scenes emerge year after year, with sugar maple and mountain-ash leading the parade of red, yellow, orange, and crimson.

West of this lookout, the trail rounds another small hill before descending into the notch between Burnt Knob and Windham High Peak. Sheltered by surrounding mountains, the notch is often calmer and warmer than nearby peaks. Strong winds rip through more exposed forests, while the notch remains still and peaceful. The sound of clashing tree limbs and whistling gusts are only background noise. Within the protected 2,900-foot notch, the trees grow straight and tall. Gray columns of sugar maple, beech, and yellow birch weave a high canopy above the soft forest floor. The notch is a sheltered, comfortable spot.

The descent from Burnt Knob into the notch is easy. Its toughest challenge is psychological. Only a little higher than Burnt Knob, Windham's summit looks undemanding before descending into the notch. Dropping into the notch adds another 400 feet of ascent. Sighs are difficult to suppress once falling into Windham's shadow. Obediently following the upward slope, the trail begins the final climb. Occasional steep spots and short, level sections add variety. The elevation piles up, and it feels like the summit must lie around the next bend. Each bend brings disappointment, and the moderate climb continues. A high elevation forest of mountain maple, striped maple, black cherry, fire cherry, and yellow birch lines the path. The wet, cool, and windy environment stunts and twists the trees. The forest canopy lowers as elevation increases. Large hobblebush patches colonize sunny habitats.

The forest parts one last time as the trail crests Windham High Peak. The summit has two scenic lookouts. The first, situated atop a large sandstone boulder, provides a 180-degree panorama of the lowlands north and east of the Catskills. North of Windham, the Helderbergs' dissected topography stretches to the Mohawk River. Albany's Empire State Plaza looms as distant white columns among the green fields and forests. The State University's five towers rise west of the city. Vermont's Green Mountains rise beyond Albany.

The Hudson River's placid blue waters flow from the Adirondacks to the Atlantic. Once past Glens Falls, the river follows a north-south line and serves as an orientation beacon. Two bridges cross the river: one for the Massachusetts Turnpike spur of the New York State Thruway, and farther south, the Rip Van Winkle Bridge connecting the city of Hudson and the Village of Catskill. Along the eastern horizon rise the Berkshires with 3,487-foot Mount Greylock towering above the range. Thick forest cover hides the Catskills' high peaks to the south. Without any other major Catskill peak in view, this lookout has a unique perspective of the surrounding valleys.

A few steps west of the summit is a south-facing overlook. Cast in a frame of fire cherry and sugar maple, this view of the Blackheads holds a pleasant mountain charm. While sugar maple do not commonly grow at this elevation, this healthy stand tops 30 feet.

After this vista, the trail begins its long descent from Windham. Retracing the trail is the shortest return route. Although many routes cross the mountain, none provide the grandeur of Burnt Knob, and this route provides an opportunity to visit Acra Point. By following the escarpment trail a half-mile east from where it parts with the return route, the trail will climb Acra Point to reveal an extraordinary view down Black Dome Valley. Windham High Peak and Burnt Knob form the valley's northern wall, while the Blackheads hold the south. Along the western horizon stand Vly and Bearpen Mountains. The reward is well worth the extra effort.

Windham High Peak marks the Catskills' northeastern extreme. At 3,524 feet, Windham is the third lowest of the Catskills' 3,500-foot peaks, but its proximity to the Hudson Valley accents its elevation. Pleasant forests, diverse vegetation, and spectacular fall color characterize the area, making it one of the country's finest autumn destinations.

THE NORTHWESTERN CATSKILLS

Unlike the eastern Catskills, which abruptly rise from the Hudson Valley, the northwestern Catskills build from the endless hills of the Allegheny Plateau. Where the plateau ends and mountains begin is a matter of opinion, but Mount Utsayantha, near Stamford, New York, is truly a Catskill Mountain. Devoured by glacial ice, the northwestern Catskills have a generic appearance. The large hills and small mountains have a less rugged character than other sections of the range. People and towns nestle between the mountains, and the lower slopes remain pastureland. The forests are young, having been cut for tanbark and other purposes. Many of the peaks reveal pastoral views of the surrounding countryside. The area includes Westkill, Bearpen, and Huntersfield Mountains, Pratt's Rocks, Grand Gorge, and a host of smaller peaks.

From above Pratt's Rocks, looking southeast at the Schoharie Valley, Vly, Balsam, Sherill, Northdome, and Pine Island

WESTKILL

Hike: Westkill
Roundtrip Hiking Distance: 6.6 miles
County and Town: Greene, Lexington
Parking: Eastern end of Westkill Valley (County Road 6)
Difficulty: moderate-difficult
Bushwhack: no
Elevation Gain: 1750 feet
Mile: 0.0: Trail begins at end of Spruceton Road (blue markers)
1.0: Diamond Notch Falls. Trail crosses bridge. Turn west (red markers)
    toward Westkill's summit.
2.4: Pass small rock cave.
3.1: Buck Ridge Lookout
3.2: Pass ledge with a northern overlook
3.3: Summit of Westkill. Return via same route
5.6: Trail junction at Diamond Notch Falls
6.6: Return to Spruceton Road parking area

Westkill Mountain, the Catskills' sixth highest peak, rises to 3,880 feet. Unlike many neighboring summits, it thrusts a distinctive outline into the sky. Westkill is a massive mountain, sprouting many spurs and ridges. Although Westkill is impressive, neighboring Hunter Mountain's 160 feet of additional elevation casts a wide shadow. Hunter's slopes often block Westkill from view or drown its profile. Centered among the north central Catskills' highest peaks, Westkill can lose its distinctive identity. Despite these drawbacks, its upper slopes hold their own charm and beauty.

Trails lead to Westkill from Lanesville and the Spruceton Valley. The Spruceton Valley trail is the shorter route and includes Diamond Notch Falls. Isolated by high mountains to the north, east, and south, Spruceton Valley is a natural fortress, open only to the west. A 2,000-

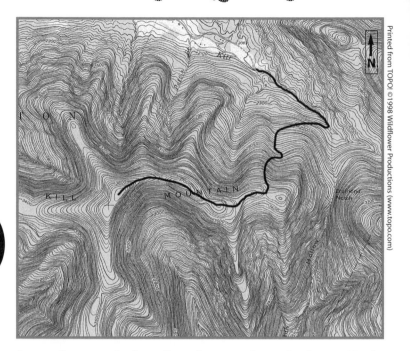

foot wall surrounds the valley. The entry is north of Deep Notch. Westkill Creek, a small, underfit tributary of Schoharie Creek, drains the valley's interior. The area's natural history parallels the Black Dome Valley; the valleys share shape, contours, and orientation.

The mountains encircling Spruceton Valley all surpass 3,200 feet, with Westkill forming the valley's southeastern wall. Only Hunter rises higher, its fire tower more than a vertical half-mile above the valley floor. Evergreen and Rusk Mountains shape the valley's northern wall. West of Westkill, Northdome, Sherill, and Balsam Mountains complete the southern wall.

Scoured and gorged by massive ice tongues, U-shaped valleys emerged when the Wisconsin Ice Sheet retreated 11,000 years ago. Overrun by continental ice sheets, the northern Catskills received a deep facelift. As ice flowed through the Schoharie Valley, a small ice tongue entered Spruceton Valley from the west. It bit deep into the vale, scraping and rounding its walls. When the ice retreated, it deposited 60-100 feet of till on the valley floor. The till hides the Catskills' stair-step topography, but till depths lessen with increasing elevation. Some mountaintops, including Westkill, have little or no till on their summits, leaving exposed bedrock ridges and the accompanying stair-step topography.

Hunter, Rusk, and Evergreen Mountains sheltered the Spruceton Valley from other ice tongues. Unable to overrun the high slopes, the ice spent its fury upon these mountains' northern slopes. On a larger scale, the northern Catskills limited the continental ice sheets' influence on the southern peaks. After the ice tongue retreated from Spruceton Valley, smaller alpine glaciers continued to shape Westkill's northern slopes. Westkill's southern face has a diverse topography mainly derived from alpine glaciers. Together, these alpine glaciers gouged steep slopes around Westkill's pointed 3,880-foot summit, creating the Catskills' only Matterhorn.

𝕩𝕩 𝕩𝕩

The trail's first mile is an old roadbed. Young yellow birch and black cherry escort the trail through the valley's eastern end. Westkill Creek parallels the path, dark hemlocks lining its banks. The trail leads into Diamond Notch, where Hunter's slopes almost touch Westkill's. The notch also separates the Esopus and Schoharie drainage basins.

As the land rises from Spruceton Valley's floor, it funnels the local drainage through Diamond Notch Falls. Westkill Creek's massing waters form this graceful fall. A 15-foot sheet of cold water charms the scene with a playful roar. Green mosses drip with moisture along the rocks. Sunlight filters through a forest of striped maple, yellow birch, and hemlock to sparkle off the rushing water and dapple the ground with highlight and shadow. Via erosion, the water removed the streambed's till and cut into the jointed bedrock. Continuously wearing into the sandstone, this fall will degrade into a cascade. Much of the water already dives along the accompanying natural staircase.

Eventually, this upstream channel will pirate the entire flow and Diamond Notch Falls will die. Oblivious to the geologic future, the stream continues its gravity-inspired trip.

The trail crosses Westkill Creek above the falls and then splits. Its southwestern branch heads for Westkill's summit, while the southeastern branch continues to Diamond Notch. Once out of the valley, the trail climbs quickly. Steep slopes present a different world than the gentle valley. The path maintains a steady, diagonal course up the mountain. Large rocks line the trail. Most of them hail from the last ice age, freed during that period's freezing and thawing episodes. Today, the process continues at a slower pace. Small environmental nudges start the broken sandstones and shales down the mountainside, and gravity never ceases in its attempts to pull down the Catskills. If no new uplift occurs, gravity will win, and the Catskills will level off into a peneplain.

Thick green foliage paints the ground wherever sunlight penetrates the canopy. Small tree stems, brown and gray, support the 30-foot canopy. Man cleared the original forest for tanbark, used the land for pasture, and later abandoned the spent slopes. Economically worthless, the tax burden beyond its value, these wasted mountain lands reverted to State ownership. In the 1880s, it became part of the Catskill State Park. Forest cover returned, but fire and erosion continued to degrade the land. Time heals these scars, and the present forest attests to the area's rebirth.

Beech, sugar maple, and hemlock dominate Westkill's lower forests. A few red spruce and planted Norway spruce join the forest. Similar in diameter and height, the largest trees attest to past wide-scale disturbances. Hemlock congregates in shady pockets on the cool, north-facing slopes. Striped maple grows well beneath the canopy, its distinctive green and white-striped bark a distinct species identifier. Hobblebush's conspicuous, large, rough leaves are common in the understory.

The trail remains steep, pressing its rapid elevation gains. Rusk Mountain's 3,680-foot summit forms the backdrop for the northern hardwood forest. Evergreen Mountain sits west of Rusk, and together

Looking northwest at the East Jewett Range, Windham High Peak, and the Blackheads these mountains define the isolated valley's northern wall. The mountains ringing Spruceton Valley insulate it from the sun's warmth and strong winds, keeping it cool and calm year round. The cool, damp conditions promote the growth of hemlock, a common species. Wood sorrel thrives on Westkill's slopes; no scene seems complete without their heart-shaped leaves. In summer, their purple and white flowers stand out against the green background. The sorrel is edible, its flavor much like lemon.

The regenerating northern hardwood forest grows in thin, rocky, and infertile soils. Often composed of hard-packed glacial till, the soils cement into fragipans, making root penetration difficult. Common throughout the Catskills, fragipans lower drainage and fertility. Agricultural productivity quickly declines in these soils, but trees can thrive since they concentrate nutrients in their biomass.

Glaciation altered the Catskills' character, changing V-shaped, water-eroded valleys into U-shaped, ice-carved ones. Without glaciation and till deposition, the Catskills would appear different. Deeper and V-shaped, the land would resemble the American southwest. Rugged cliffs, ledges, and mesas would define the land. Cold, hard formations would replace the Catskills' soft mountain charm.

After a long and strenuous climb into a subalpine forest, the trail levels along Westkill's 3,400-foot backbone. Balsam fir, along with a few upper hardwoods and red spruce, dominate the forest. Black cherry, fire cherry, paper birch, and mountain-ash are the most common hardwoods. Balsam perfumes the boreal forest air. A spongy mix of brown needles, branches, and leaves cover the forest floor. Slices of sky hint at extensive vistas; however, the forest never parts to reveal the surrounding country.

After an easy, westerly ridgetop walk, the trail begins to lift. As it gains elevation, the path passes a small cave. Actually a sandstone overhang, this small hollow disappoints the adventurous. The trail then passes the 3,500-foot line. Designed to protect and preserve the Catskills' high elevation environments, this line marks the upper limit for camping and fires. Once above this elevation, the trail becomes steeper. Westkill's prize vista, Buck Ridge Lookout, is the next landmark. The spectacular view opens from an exposed sandstone ledge 80 feet below the summit.

The sun-warmed ledge is the perfect place to spend an afternoon. Situated at the head of a cirque, the mountain's contours flow southeast. The cirque was a last haven for a retreating ice age. A stream of ice slowly flowed from this frozen reservoir into the Chichester Valley. A spectacular, 180-degree southeast-centered view opens from atop this ice-carved landscape. A forest of red spruce, balsam fir, paper birch, black cherry, and mountain-ash frame Buck Ridge Lookout. To the northeast lies Rusk's shoulder, and beyond it is 3,524-foot Windham High Peak. The almost 4,000-foot Blackhead Range also lifts to the northeast.

Onteora Mountain and East Jewett Range, both heavily eroded during the ice age, lie between higher mountains to the north and south. The dwarfed peaks barely reach 3,000 feet. Located in the Schoharie Valley, they received the continental ice sheets' direct impact, losing more stature than their partially-shielded neighbors.

Hunter's northwestern slopes and Colonel's Chair hold the northeastern foreground. The ski slopes orient the mountain scene. Hunter's 4,040-foot summit soars east of Westkill. The southeastern scene features 3,440-foot Olderbark Mountain jutting from Plateau Mountain's partially hidden slopes. Overlook Mountain's 3,150-foot summit soars along the eastern horizon, its 300-foot transmission tower visible to sharp eyes. A small slice of the Ashokan Reservoir fills the basin to the east-southeast. Westkill's southeastern slopes fall into Chichester Creek's turbulent depths. Mount Tremper and Carl Mountains complete the southeastern foreground, while 2,300-foot Mount Sheridan, one of the lowest peaks visible, hides Phoenicia.

Wittenberg and Cornell Mountains rise to the south. To their southeast is High Point and its distinctive twin ledges. Slide Mountain, the Catskills' highest peak, rises west of them. Hidden in front of Slide's 4,180-foot mass is 3,200-foot Giant Ledge and 3,720-foot Panther Mountain.

A few steps above Buck Ridge Lookout, the trail opens onto a north-facing view. The vista is less extensive than the Buck Ridge Lookout. Since it faces north into the enclosed valley, it is cooler, a result of the air trapped in Spruceton Valley and the lack of direct sunlight. The environmental differences foster a healthy and vigorous spruce-fir forest.

The northern lookout overlooks Spruceton Valley. Rusk and Evergreen Mountains compose the foreground. Huntersfield Mountain's 3,423-foot summit marches into the northern horizon. To the northwest, 2,700-foot Tower Mountain, another ice age victim, squats in the Schoharie Valley.

The trail continues at a gentle slope once above the lookouts. The summit comes quickly and without fanfare. No views open from the spruce-fir-clad peak. The path then descends to the west and heads back to the Spruceton Valley a few miles west of the trail's entry into Diamond Notch. It is a long and uneventful trip. The waterfall's allure and a return to Buck Ridge Lookout make backtracking a better option.

BEARPEN

Hike: Bearpen
Roundtrip Hiking Distance: 6.6 miles
County and Town: Greene, Prattsville
Parking: Off County Road 2, 4.5 miles from intersection with Route 23A (park along road, access trail is a red dirt road on the north side of road)
Difficulty: moderate
Bushwhack: no
Elevation Gain: 1600 feet
(unmarked trail follows an old dirt road)
Mile: 0.0: Trail begins along Greene County Route 2 (accessible from NY Route 23A)
3.0: Pass small pond
3.2: Reach top of old ski slopes
3.3: Summit of Bearpen, return by same route
6.6: Return to parking area

The Catskill Mountains extend westward from the Hudson Valley as lines of stalwart peaks. The mountain ridges split as they head west, forming two groups. The main mass pulls south, centering on Slide Mountain. To the north runs the escarpment and the high ridges surrounding the Schoharie Valley. More than 40 miles from the Hudson River, Bearpen Mountain, the final Catskill peak reaching 3,500 feet, rises in Greene County. Although a large mountain, its nondescript slopes meld into the neighboring peaks.

Directly exposed to the invading continental ice sheets, Bearpen's rounded slopes have few topographic distractions. Its slopes are smooth and even. Few ridges protrude from its backbone, leaving the mountain without a distinct character. Ice age erosion scraped and scoured the rough edges into sands, silts, and clays. When the last ice sheet retreated, it deposited a thick till on the mountain. The result is a large,

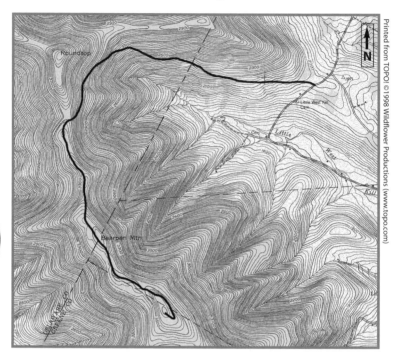

featureless hill. Despite the heavy erosion, Bearpen's summit reaches 3,600 feet.

While Bearpen Mountain has a generic appearance, the mountain's history, successional ecology, and scenic beauty give it character. Wide views to the north and east reveal the surrounding countryside. Easy slopes and wide trails make Bearpen's summit accessible.

Bearpen lines the Schoharie Valley's southern side. The trail begins south of a small parking area along Greene County Route 2. Situated among farmland and open fields, Bearpen curls around and forms the southern skyline. After defining the summit, the high ridge falls into a notch and then rises as Vly Mountain.

In the 1960s, a small ski center operated on Bearpen's northeastern face. The cut trails, still visible, are no longer open. Through forest succession, a young northern hardwood forest is reclaiming Bearpen's disturbed landscapes. Farming, grazing, and logging also helped remove Bearpen's mature forest communities.

An abandoned hard-packed dirt road forms the trail. The packed red clay path follows the mountain's semicircular backbone to the summit. The path begins at a gentle incline, lined with fields of young trees and old rock walls. Recently farmland, these fields support bushy white pines, quaking aspen, and hosts of wildflowers. A rainbow of floral color accents the blue-green needles and shimmering leaves.

When light breezes caress the air, the aspen leaves shake on their slender petioles, filling the forest with random motion. Pine and aspen shade the open meadows, the first major step in forest succession. The journey through these evolving fields heads into the middle stages of succession. Since each forest generation alters the environment, long abandoned areas have larger trees and different species.

After walking a short distance through the fields, the landscape changes to a young woodland, and forest composition reflects the shadier conditions. Leaves and needles familiar from the fields share the slopes with red maple, witch hazel, staghorn sumac, paper birch, northern red oak, and black cherry. Only a few decades earlier, this forest was also an open field. Plentiful sunlight favored the first growth of pine and aspen. In open conditions, they grow faster and stronger than other species, but since they are intolerant of shade, their seeds cannot grow without direct sunlight. Even in the shade of their parents, these species cannot survive, but their small seeds can blow to distant sites. Some will be lucky and settle in open, sunny areas. Most never sprout.

Beneath the pioneers, seeds tolerant of light shade drive the forest's evolution. The second generation—often red maple, striped maple, black cherry, and northern red oak—eventually join, and then displace, the canopy's pioneers.

Documentation from the early 1800s shows that trees of late successional stages—sugar maple, beech, yellow birch, and hemlock—covered the Catskills. After generations of succession and a disturbance-free environment, these shade-tolerant species will again dominate Bearpen's slopes. The forest and soil will mature and the canopy will shade the ground, allowing the soil to retain additional moisture and decreasing sunlight so only shade-tolerant species can survive. Unlike pioneers, these varieties can grow in their parents' shade, so the forest can attain a steady state. A few slender stems of these shade-tolerant species already mix with the recovering forest.

Most trees on Bearpen's lower slopes are less than a few decades old. Among the adolescent trees, a set of mature sugar maple line the path. Popular with farmers for form and function, sugar maples provide shade, beauty, and maple syrup. The maples cooled the roadway and separated it from fields of corn, hay, and cows. An image of the past, these trees memorialize an almost forgotten lifestyle.

Despite the forest's rebirth, signs of man's past activities remain. Well-constructed stone walls, built with rocks removed from the fields, mark abandoned pastures and property lines. No longer needed, they are another monument to the area's agricultural past.

The path maintains a gentle incline as it winds along Bearpen's lower slopes. Man's past uses slowly fade into history as the trail moves deeper into the forest. Tree age and species diversity continue to increase. Shagbark hickory, an uncommon Catskill inhabitant, makes a distinctive appearance. Long vertical strips of bark lift from the silvery-gray trunks. Stands of Norway spruce, planted in the 1930s by the Civilian Conservation Corps to help the forest return, create solid blocks of dark foliage. Often cut for timber, Norway spruce, a European native, grows well in the Catskills, but reproduces poorly.

An occasional white oak interrupts the masses of young trees, spreading its massive crown above the juvenile forest. Akin to the large sugar maples, these oaks are another part of a lost world. A favorite of farmers, white oak are unpalatable to livestock, mature quickly, and provide summer shade. Oaks thrive in open fields free from light competition, their twisted limbs spreading in all directions. The low, rounded form increases stability and resistance to wind damage.

In abandoned fields, the sprawling pasture trees have a head start over new growth. Crowded by neighboring stems, the young forest will grow up, rather than out, and after a few decades the invading

An east-facing vista reveals Huntersfield Mountain and the Helderberg Mountains

trees will shade the older oaks. Since the oaks spent their lives without competition for light, they cannot adjust to the new conditions. Shaded branches die quickly. Soon, the second-growth forest overtops the field trees, and without direct sunlight they deteriorate into wooden heirlooms. Within a half-century, the open field oaks are no more.

The young, dense forest supports little undergrowth. The air is cool and calm. Dead leaves are the only ground cover. Starved for light, the sun-loving field plants die once the young trees shade the ground. Occasional patches of grass, remnants from the old fields, carpet the forest floor despite the dim environment. Ferns and flowers are rare. No shrubs grow beneath the canopy.

The undeveloped understory is a combination of two factors. The first is the forest's dense canopy. The solid weave of wood and leaves allows only a muted light to reach the ground. Time is the second factor. The decades this land spent as open fields eliminated their seed banks. Seeds from sun-loving plants cannot survive in the dark conditions, so there is no understory. In a few decades, this will change as seeds from shade-tolerant species migrate into the area.

In contrast with the thick forest, the trail creates a sunny slash. The trailside environment is hotter and drier than the woods. Bathed with plentiful sunlight, the trailside community is a thick, tangled border. Goldenrod, pinks, grasses, white wood asters, and other common field plants escort the trail.

The path maintains its easy pace while the forest continues to change. Abandoned longer than the slopes below, older trees dominate these stands. Unlike the masses of young stems, these trees average 40 feet in height. The species also change. Northern red oak and blue-beech create an atypical Catskill forest community. The broken canopy allows light to mottle the ground. Ferns and flowers capitalize on the additional light resources. A young understory of sugar maple, beech, and striped maple grows beneath the oaks. After a brief tenure in the canopy, the oaks will disappear. Oaks thrive in strong sunlight, but the northern hardwoods grow best in shaded environments. The shade prevents oak reproduction, and the field oaks perish. Only a large scale disturbance will provide the needed sunlight for additional oaks to grow. If undisturbed, these oaks will remain kings of this stand for the next 200 years before yielding to the northern hardwoods.

The flowers and grasses sprouting along the trail are a sharp contrast to the dark forest floor. White snakeroot—safe for cows to eat, but a poison to humans—abounds. Many a tragedy occurred when tainted milk passed the poison to unsuspecting people. Farmers regularly clear their fields of this plant. A less dangerous plant, New York aster, provides purple and yellow trailside highlights. Yellow jewelweed also thrives along the sunny lane.

Elevation increases as the trail traces Bearpen's loping profile. With a sudden thrust, slope increases. Small rock outcrops protrude from the smooth till layer. The forest takes on an upland character, favoring trees suited for harsh conditions. Tree height decreases, stunted by cold and persistent winds. Among the new dominant species are black cherry and yellow birch.

Understory changes reflect the increasing elevation. Bearpen's middle and upper slopes support hordes of blackberry and raspberry bushes. Sun-loving pioneers, these prickly shrubs line the trail. Blackberries boldly display their fruit while the softer, sweeter raspberries hide beneath the leaves. Both make delicious treats.

As the trail approaches Bearpen's top ridge, light gray sandstone outcrops cap the landscape. Shallow and poorly-drained soils keep the terrain wet and muddy. Large pools of water are common on the glacially-engineered slopes. Wind, a constant force here, twists and dwarfs the trees. Most introduced plant species cannot grow at these high elevations, creating native gardens. The yellow birch and black cherry construct a broken canopy complimented by an understory of hobblebush, blackberry, striped maple, and mountain maple. Soft ferns and high grasses sway in the mountain breezes.

Geographic changes match the environmental alterations. The trail begins in the Schoharie Valley, part of Greene County. As it moves west, the path enters Delaware County for a mile before returning to Greene County and Bearpen's top ridge.

A series of small ridges create Bearpen's summit. A large pond lined with stunted trees lies near the mountaintop and paints a pretty scene. Bearpen's upper elevations are poorly-drained, and puddles are everywhere. The next small series of rises leads to drier terrain and brings the trail to the summit, where the flat peak extends to the southeast following the mountain's backbone. Few large trees grow along the windswept peak, opening many partial views. The old ski trails, visible from the parking area, blend with the recovering forest. Extensive vistas peer east from the top of these forgotten runs.

The northeastern Catskills are the backdrop for the view from Bearpen's summit. Continental ice sheets and the Schoharie Creek carved the northwest-trending valley. The ice is gone, but the water remains at work. Both the underfit stream and the U-shaped valley reflect their glacial heritage. Downstream, the Schoharie Creek flows into the Schoharie Reservoir, part of New York City's water supply. Huntersfield Mountain's eye-catching slopes rise east of the reservoir. The isolated, 3,423-foot peak towers over the nearby lower hills.

Huntersfield leads east to the northeastern escarpment. Pisgah, Hayden, Zoar, and in the distance, 3,524-foot Windham High Peak, sit atop this ridge.

Cave Mountain, home to Ski Windham, and Tower Mountain eclipse Windham's eastern slopes. Patterson Ridge, a low mountain north of the Schoharie Valley, brings the view back to Bearpen. South of Windham is 3,940-foot Thomas Cole Mountain. Left of Thomas Cole are the East Jewett Range and Onteora Mountain, glacially-worn peaks barely reaching 3,000 feet. Beyond them rise Kaaterskill High Peak and Roundtop. Hunter Mountain, marked by its ski trails and partially hidden by Bearpen's vegetation, thrusts above the Schoharie Valley. Rusk, Evergreen, and Pine Island Mountains frame the southeastern foreground.

From Bearpen's summit, distinct topographical patterns appear within the northern Catskills. Huntersfield, Windham, and Thomas Cole Mountains resemble triplets. Similar rocks, positions, time scale, and long-term environmental conditions created this repetition. As continental ice sheets moved up the Schoharie Valley, they collided with each mountain at the same angle, producing parallel structures. The foreground mountains—Cave, Tower, Onteora, and the East Jewett Range—received the ice sheets' full impact, losing their character and upper elevations in the icy onslaught.

Bearpen's southern face reveals another view. Belleayre and its ski trails set the foreground, the wide peak sporting tiger stripes. Beyond Belleayre are the western Catskills' highest peaks: Doubletop, Graham, and Balsam Lake Mountains. Dry Brook Ridge trails northwest from Balsam Lake Mountain. Bearpen's western face has another limited view. It overlooks the smaller of the Catskills' two Batavia Kill Valleys. Plattekill Mountain and its ski center stand out among the western Catskills' high hills. A limited northern view includes Shultice and Irish Mountains, the Moresville Range, and Mount Utsayantha, the Catskills' northwestern cornerstone. The Helderbergs define the northern horizon.

Vistas from Bearpen's flat summit hold less fanfare than most Catskill vistas. Limited by the small ledge and scrubby mountaintop vegetation, scenery yields to the recovering forest. Bearpen Mountain provides a different experience than the better-known peaks to the south, southwest, and east. Bearpen is a window to the hills, low mountains, and farmlands coating the western Catskills. Its frontier location and easy access provides a great place for a pleasant adventure.

From near the parking area of Bearpen, looking south towards Vly

HUNTERSFIELD

Hike: Huntersfield
Roundtrip Hiking Distance: 2.4 miles
County and Town: Greene, Ashland-Prattsville
Parking: Small pull-off at crest of Huntersfield Road
Difficulty: easy-moderate
Bushwhack: no
Elevation Gain: 600 feet
Mile: 0.0 Begin hike at small pass along Huntersfield Road
    1.1 Reach loop that surrounds the summit—follow north spur
    1.4 Return to start of the loop
    2.4 Return to parking area

Isolated from the Catskills' higher summits and surrounded by undersized mountains, Huntersfield Mountain stalwartly lifts into the northern Catskill skyline. Although it would pale in comparison if placed next to any of the Catskills' highest peaks, Huntersfield's location in the northwestern Catskills marks it as a beacon of elevation. To the north the land softens, graced by the Helderberg Mountains' gentle, rounded forms and wide valleys. To the east and west run the Catskills' northernmost summits, but few of them reach 3,000 feet. Only to the south are the mountains higher.

Smashed and smothered by glaciers, Huntersfield does not have many topographical features. Small alpine glaciers gouged cirques into the summit—one for each cardinal direction. As a result Huntersfield's peak stands like a giant "X" among the mountain masses. When viewed from the surrounding valleys, however, Huntersfield is not a distinctive landform.

Huntersfield Mountain is not part of the Catskill Park, and the mountain's character is not pristine—the forests are young, often second and third growth. Although owned by the State, the area is open to more intense recreational and economic use than its sister peaks within

Catskill Park. To encourage recreation, the State has improved access, manufactured views, and built a lean-to atop this relatively unknown peak. A decaying, rutted dirt road winds through the unending pickets of small trees, ascending almost to the summit. From there, newly constructed trails complete the journey, providing an ease of access not available for decades. The walk to Huntersfield is appropriate for beginning hikers, but the views from the top make it worthwhile for anyone interested in the Catskill Mountains. Only the last quarter-mile, where the trail climbs the steep "X," does the route become difficult.

Like many Catskill trails, the path to Huntersfield begins along a red-colored dirt road. The trail passes through an abandoned quarry, taking an east-facing bearing that it follows for the entire hike. A young mixed-hardwood forest covers the slopes—mainly American beech, black cherry, yellow birch, big-tooth aspen, and northern red oak—a typical Catskill blend on recovering slopes. An occasional older tree squats among the growing horde of slender stems.

Man heavily used most of Huntersfield's lower elevations. Timber was cut for firewood, construction, and the leather tanning industry; sheep and cattle grazed the open slopes; and crops were grown where the slopes were gentle enough. By the early 1900s, the mountain's resources were depleted and its natural functions lay in ruin.

During the 1930s, workers with the Civilian Conservation Corps helped restore areas like Huntersfield Mountain. The CCC planted new forests, mainly red pine, Norway spruce, and tamarack—species that grew quickly and would produce a new timber crop. Over time, however, man's philosophy and economic outlook for the Catskills changed, allowing the trees to grow and mature far beyond the CCC's original intent. As a result, many mature groves of single tree species dominate Huntersfield's lower slopes. Unfortunately, the monocultures and non-native species do not provide as high quality habitat as the native northern hardwood forests they replaced.

Despite the lack of variety employed in reforesting Huntersfield, the mountain's proximity to the low elevation valleys to the north enhances its diversity. The blending of the valley's mixed hardwoods with the Catskills' northern hardwood forest increases the number of

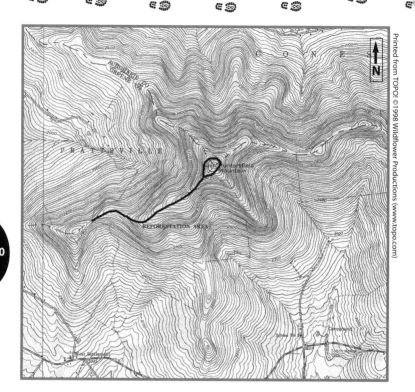

species that can find food and shelter. The mountain's position, shielded from the storms that approach from the south, reduces the amount of precipitation it receives relative to most other Catskill peaks. As a result, wherever there are well-drained soils, a strong contingent of oak trees is likely to thrive.

When hiking on Huntersfield, mud and standing water biases the hike and the environment. The glacially inspired landscape does not drain well, and the standing water influences the plant life. Species unable to tolerate the flooded conditions can only survive on the steeper, better-drained slopes. Oak and beech fall into this category. The birch and some of the maples and aspen are more tolerant of the waterlogged soils.

Huntersfield Mountain and its recovering forests are a good place to note the Catskills' avian population. Birds play an important role in nature, and are often the Catskills' most conspicuous animal life. Birds aid in plant pollination, distribute seeds, limit insect and rodent populations, and are a food source for some reptiles and mammals. Some bird species are resident, remaining in the Catskills year-round. Black-capped chickadees, white-breasted nuthatches, downy woodpeckers, and tufted titmice stay for the winter and live off the cold season's limited fare.

Most of the Catskills' bird species migrate south for the winter. The insects and seeds smaller birds eat are available throughout the year in the tropics. Most raptors such as Cooper's and sharp-shinned hawks tend to migrate to the southeastern United States. All of the species return north to reproduce, using the growing season's bounty to nurture their young. While hikers often traverse two or three miles to reach their destination, the Catskills' migratory birds trek for thousands of miles to reach theirs.

The Catskills lie along the Atlantic Flyway. This highway in the sky for migratory birds stretches from the Arctic to South America. Huntersfield Mountain, among the highest points directly south of the Mohawk Valley, attracts many migratory birds and its location adjacent to lower elevation habitats makes it a popular nesting area. As a result, many birds visit or live on this peak each year. Early mornings, especially in spring, make for the best birding outings, and quite a few species can be seen or heard along the trail.

The red-eyed vireo is one of the most common birds found in the Catskills. Its bold song proclaims, "here I am, over here." During the spring and summer breeding season they sing all day, even while foraging. The red-eyed vireo is common throughout the Appalachian Mountains, with up to one pair nesting per acre. Each year they migrate to South America, where their main food source, insects, remain abundant.

Another common migratory bird found in the Catskills is the brown creeper. Small and reclusive, these birds usually nest between the bark and trunk on a dead or dying tree. Brown creepers usually

A northwestern vista shows off the Catskills' northwesternmost high peaks

make a soft lisping call as they slowly work their way up a tree looking for food. They only ascend trees; once at the top they fly to the base of another tree and begin anew. As they climb, they use their stiff tail for support. They eat insects such as caterpillars, katydids, and leafhoppers. Brown creepers migrate to the southeastern United States during the winter, but a few may remain year-round.

Yellow-bellied sapsuckers, among the quietest of migrating woodpeckers, frequent Huntersfield's slopes, preferring stream-side forests and its mixed hardwood-conifer stands. They drill lines of parallel holes in their favorite trees, often poplars or basswood, licking the sap and eating the insects in and around the holes. Unfortunately for the trees, these holes often expose the trunk to disease. Ants are the yellow-bellied sapsucker's major source of food, but they also eat wasps, beetles, and seeds. They usually nest in trees with rotted heartwoods. They will return to the same tree each year, but will excavate a new hole. Of the tree species found on Huntersfield, aspen, birch, beech, and maple are their favorite nesting sites.

As the trail snakes toward Huntersfield, it reveals occasional glimpses of the summit, providing an indication of the remaining distance. Once near the summit, the dirt road wanders into a small, level glade. From there, a narrow foot-trail begins its outline of the peak. Oak, birch, and cherry trees cover the area. Blackberries and striped maple are common in the understory. The views from Huntersfield, despite being slashed into existence by power tools, provide some unique and impressive Catskill vistas. A few steps along the trail's northern branch delivers a wide, north-centered vista. Twisted branches frame the western theater, providing a heavy foreground for the Catskills' northwestern peaks. Vly, Bearpen, Roundtop, the Mooresville Range, Irish Mountain, and Utsayantha march toward the western horizon. To the north are scores of rounded hills and deep, often parallel, stream valleys. Both fall into the Mohawk Valley. On a clear day, the Adirondacks' sturdy forms poke into the northern skyline. Albany's white towers gleam in the sunlight. Far to the northeast lift Vermont's Green Mountains, but on most days they barely show in the haze-filled distance.

The trail wraps around the 3,423-foot summit before entering another artificial clearing. Devoid of the flat ledges common to the rest of the mountain, the soils here are better drained. From the clearing, which is about 30 feet lower than the summit, the land falls sharply to the south. A lean-to stands atop the conquered slope, providing guests with a beautiful, albeit rectangular, view southward. Despite being more than 30 miles away, Slide Mountain dominates the view. The cut forest track leads the eye to the 4,180-foot king of the Catskills. Closer to Huntersfield runs one of the northern Catskills' major ridgelines that includes Rusk, Hunter, and Westkill Mountains.

Once the trail completes its loop around the summit, the return route follows the dirt road used to approach Huntersfield. Except for the mud, it is an easy walk, providing time to enjoy the recovering forest and its resident wildlife. Huntersfield Mountain may not be one of the Catskills' highest or best-known peaks, but it is one of its most accessible and recreation-friendly mountains, perfect for an afternoon or weekend of pleasant adventure.

PRATT'S ROCKS

Hike: Pratt's Rocks
Roundtrip Hiking Distance:
County and Town: Greene, Prattsville
Parking: Route 23A, just east of Prattsville (at a picnic area)
Difficulty: moderate (but short)
Bushwhack: no
Elevation Gain: 650 feet
Mile: 0.0: Begin at parking area along NY Route 23
      0.2: Reach Pratt's Rocks, continue east along ridge-line trail
      0.4: Reach open ledges, return by same route
      0.8: Return to parking area

Prattsville nestles alongside the Schoharie Creek in Greene County's northwestern corner. Sleepy by today's standards, this small town boomed with life as a major leather-tanning center in the mid-1800s. Founded by Zadock Pratt, his tannery became the United State's largest. In 1836 and 1842, he was elected as a United States Congressman. Mr. Pratt's tanneries made him rich and powerful, but he was better known for his eccentricities.

Pratt's Rocks began as a barter. Around 1865, a traveling stone-cutter offered his services in exchange for housing. Mr. Pratt accepted, employing the stonecutter to shape the coarse sandstones overlooking the Schoharie Valley. Pratt's love for horses—he owned more than 1,000 well-bred animals—and hemlock trees, his source of wealth, were the inspiration for this monument. He liked the results and hired additional carvers to chisel, polish, and shape the rock to his standards. Stone benches allowed Pratt and his guests to sit and enjoy the carvings and surrounding Catskill Mountain scenery. Never completed, the work continued until Pratt's death in 1880. Among the unfinished works was his proposed tomb.

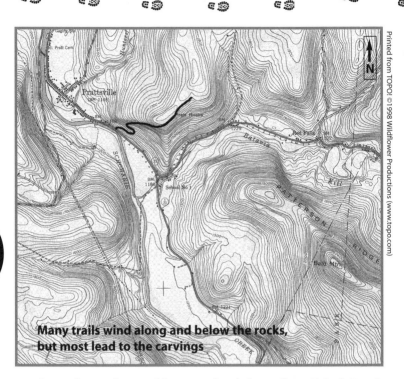

Printed from TOPO! ©1998 Wildflower Productions (www.topo.com)

Many trails wind along and below the rocks, but most lead to the carvings

Located east of town, this exposed rock face reflects Zadock Pratt's life. Alongside the horse and hemlock is the family coat of arms and a carving of his son, a Union officer killed in the Civil War. His son's death devastated Pratt, and the stone likeness became an obsession. Weathered inscriptions accompany each carving, but are difficult to read.

A small pavilion along Route 23, Prattsville's main street, commemorates Pratt's Rocks. Displays transcribe the faded inscriptions and tell of the famous tanner's life. A picnic area and a small trail network lead to the stonework. The trails lead to a light gray sandstone cliff face. Chiseled stone distinguishes the rock wall. Protective white paint coats and preserves the carvings. Stone benches offer seating, but little comfort.

The vertical rock face provides a limited view, but small trees block most of it. Uncut for a few decades, this young forest replaces the open vista seen by Zadock Pratt and his guests. Limited cutting keeps the carvings' foreground clear. The youthful forest resembles those dominating the Catskills in the 1880s and 1890s. The decimated hemlock forests began to recover, with sugar maple, beech, and hemlock saplings creating a new forest. The second-growth saplings became the raw materials for a short-lived barrel hoop industry. With the hemlock supply exhausted and the tanneries out of business, it revived the regional economy. Once cut and split lengthwise, laborers bent the saplings into hoops, but in less than a decade this industry ended with the development of inexpensive metal barrel hoops.

Pratt's Rocks' current forest is a mix of beech, sugar maple, northern red oak, black cherry, and hemlock. In the picnic area, towering white pines provide a glimpse of a forested era long past. Gracefully they reach into the sky, recalling a time when thousands of 120-foot white pines lined the Catskills. Most disappeared as the long, straight, and flexible wood became masts for British and American ships. In colonial times, every white pine was the King's property. It was illegal to cut or sell one without the crown's permission.

Hamilton sandstones, a resistant rock, compose Pratt's Rocks; however, the large, uniform grains provide less strength than those on the Catskills' higher peaks. The less resistant rocks yielded the western Catskills' wide valleys and soft slopes. Mini-caverns pock the poorly-cemented rock. The loose-fitting particles left space between the rock's grains. A little rubbing can change the sandstone into a sandy grit.

After the short walk to Pratt's Rocks, the trail continues past the light gray cliff to a series of overlooks. The trail ends along private land, at a group of southeast-facing ledges with a pleasant view of the Schoharie Valley and the northwestern Catskills' highest peaks. Westkill Mountain, at 3,880 feet, is the highest point visible. Rusk and Evergreen Mountains stand north of Westkill. Together, these peaks encircle Spruceton Valley. West of the valley is Deep Notch, which rises into Halcott and Vly Mountains. Bearpen Mountain lies directly south of Pratt's Rocks. In fall, this scene explodes with color.

The combination of history and scenery at Pratt's Rocks provides a pleasant outing. On these slopes, yesterday's Catskills, full of hemlock, tanneries, and horses, meets today's second-growth forests, dairy farms, and peaceful towns. A short walk in space is a longer one in time. Above it all are beautiful spots to sit and watch the world.

A horse and a hemlock tree, the core of Pratt's wealth and pride, were the first carvings made at Pratt's Rocks

THE NORTHWESTERN CATSKILLS

In the northwestern Catskills, Bearpen Mountain is the last summit lifting above 3,500 feet, but this numerical distinction does not mark the Catskills' demise. A series of rounded ridges and peaks stretch west-northwest from Bearpen. Their glacially-sculpted lobes separate the U-shaped, underfit valleys of Schoharie Creek and the Delaware River. Water slipping to the south travels to Philadelphia, while that going north will visit New York City. The high ridge is in Greene and Delaware Counties. Lands north of it lie in Schoharie County.

Softer than the Catskills' eastern ridges, the pastoral landscape reveals distinct regional facets. The wild forests common throughout the eastern Catskills do not blanket these mountains. Pastures and fields dominate the mountains' lower elevations, and local forests are little more than even-aged woodlots. Although similar to Bearpen, Halcott, Vly, and their neighboring mountains, the history, geology, ecology, and topography create a unique natural history. Dairy farms and small towns reflect the area's peaceful, comfortable atmosphere. Man and nature interact differently among these soft slopes and wide valleys. While not a mountain wilderness, this tamed Catskill environment has its own merits. An exploration of the area expands and enhances the overall Catskill Mountain experience. Rich in history, nature, and natural history, the area holds a story not found among the Catskills' higher peaks.

Five mountains comprise this range's backbone. The best known is Mount Utsayantha, the northwesternmost Catskill peak topping 3,000 feet. Once north and west of Utsayantha's summit, elevations fall sharply. The Helderbergs and the Mohawk Valley lie to the north. The Allegheny Plateau's rolling hills fill the western landscape. Between Bearpen and Utsayantha are Roundtop, Shultice, and Irish Mountains, the Moresville Range, and McGregor Mountain. The old Susquehanna Trail (New York Route 23) parallels the range. Set in the Schoharie Valley, this route traces the mountain's northern fringe and provides access to New York's interior.

The ridge is the drainage divide between the Delaware River's headwaters and the Schoharie Basin. Headwater streams rush southwest to form the East and West Branches of the Delaware River. Grand Gorge holds the headwaters for the East Branch. The Schoharie Creek flows west, contoured by the ridge until Prattsville. Marked by a series of nick points (small watercourse drops created by continental adjustments), after Prattsville the wide mountain stream turns north for the Gilboa Reservoir and Mohawk River. Along the way, it gathers the small tributaries draining the ridge's northern face.

Mount Utsayantha and Grand Gorge—the notch separating Irish Mountain and the Moresville Range—are the area's most distinctive natural features. Unlike elsewhere in the Catskills, these features are near roads, making them easily accessible. The ridge's other mountains and notches resemble Mount Utsayantha and Grand Gorge, but have less definition and character.

Heavy glaciation and subsequent ice dams during the last ice age carved Grand Gorge and the surrounding terrain. Steep U-shaped slopes, characteristic of ice-carved areas, outline the gorge. Continental ice sheets plowed into this notch, their momentum reworking the land without mercy. The mountains patiently waited, and in time the ice sheet retreated, leaving a newly-carved world and a new blanket of till. As New York's Route 30 heads into the gorge, the steep mountain masses close about the roadway, constricting the landscape's profile into an hourglass.

The till-covered, depressed terrain at the notch's center drains poorly. Water from the neighboring mountains collects in this depression. A swamp results. Local vegetation, including red maple, hemlock, and spruce, have adaptations for wet, acidic, and oxygen-poor soils. The slow draining swamplands are the source of the East Branch of the Delaware River.

MOUNT UTSAYANTHA

Hike: Utsayantha
Roundtrip Hiking Distance: depends on route, 0-2.7 miles
County and Town: Delaware, Stamford
Parking: At top and bottom of mountain (lower parking in town of Stamford)
Difficulty: easy to moderate-difficult (depending on route)
Bushwhack: no
Elevation Gain: depends on route, up to 1350 feet
(a dirt road open to vehicle traffic)
Mile: 0.0: Follow Mountain Avenue (off NY Route 23) to dirt road ascending Utsayantha
1.2: Summit of Utsayantha

The Northwestern Catskills:
most are trail-less

Mount Utsayantha is 4.5 miles west of Grand Gorge. Its summit reaches 3,214 feet. Well-worn, the rounded mountain shows the effect of glacial scouring. Without the protruding shoulders and steep ridges common to the southeastern Catskills, Utsayantha's lower slopes make good pasture land. A maturing northern hardwood forest covers the higher elevations. Towers, overlooks, and hang glider launch pads sit atop the summit. Utsayantha's management is an exercise in multiple use.

A dirt road leads to the peak. The bumpy, but passable drive provides the easiest and quickest ascent. Hiking trails roam the fields and forests. Upon its arrival at the summit, the footpath merges with the red dirt road. The mix of man and nature on Utsayantha makes the drive feel appropriate.

Utsayantha's grassy summit is a large, level clearing. A hang glider platform launches from the mountain's northwestern face, its wooden ramp carving an open vista overlooking Stamford, the surrounding

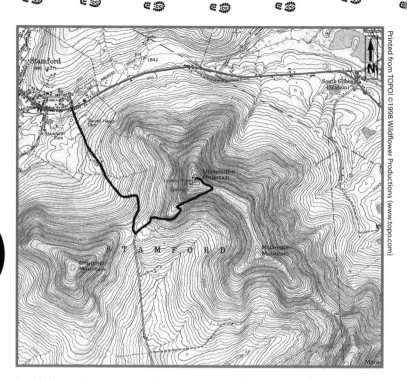

low hills, and generous valleys. Two sturdy buildings and five telecommunications towers crown the summit, adding another 60 feet to the mountain. The steel and aluminum fire tower, with its 360-degree view, is the most useful.

A climb up the sturdy tower eliminates the forest clutter, but not the neighboring towers' framework. Despite these silver spires, a spectacular view fills the horizon. Ridges and soft summits fill the western theater. The city of Oneonta nestles in the Susquehanna's underfit valley. To the north, the Helderbergs' low rounded hills line the Mohawk Valley, and the Adirondacks define the horizon. The Helderbergs continue northeast toward Vermont and the Green Mountains. Mount Greylock, Massachusetts' highest point, is most prominent among the distant peaks. A lower set of hills, the Berkshires, lead into Connecticut.

Nearby Catskill peaks dominate the eastern view. Huntersfield Mountain forms the foreground. Farther north, the eastern escarpment, Richmond Mountain, Ashland Pinnacle, Pisgah Mountain, and Zoar Mountain taper the landscape. Windham High Peak rises behind Huntersfield Mountain, while Cave and Tower Mountains fill the remaining foreground. South of Windham rise the Blackhead Range and the Kaaterskill High Peak-Roundtop massif.

The high ridge, spanning from Bearpen Mountain to Utsayantha, flows into the Catskills' main mass. Each intermediate peak is lower than Utsayantha, allowing it to overlook the entire ridge. After reaching Bearpen, the ridge continues as Vly Mountain. The land then falls into Deep Clove's shadowy depths. Balsam, Sherill, Northdome, and Westkill Mountains stand across the clove. North of them are Pine Island, Evergreen and Rusk Mountains.

Hunter Mountain forms Spruceton Valley's eastern wall, its bulk halting glacial advances within the valley and eclipsing the Devil's Path from view. Slide Mountain, the Catskills' highest peak, dominates the southern scene. The central Catskills radiate from this benchmark. To its south is Table Mountain's flat summit. West of Slide, a high ridge upholds Eagle, Big Indian, Doubletop, Graham, and Balsam Lake Mountains. Atop Balsam Lake Mountain are the dark, foreboding fir stands supplying its name.

Glaciation played a major role in shaping the ridge holding Mount Utsayantha, Grand Gorge, and the surrounding mountains. As the Catskills' northernmost mountain ridge, it received the full erosional power of each ice sheet. Like ocean waves crashing onto shore, mile-thick glaciers and subsequent advances plowed into the area's northern slopes. Ridges and summits crumbled beneath the ice, losing hundreds of feet in elevation. Protruding spurs ceased to exist. When the ice sheets retreated, till-covered slopes emerged. During the last glacial advances—the Wagon Wheel and Grand Gorge advances—ice overran this area. Unlike the southern Catskills, alpine glaciation left few marks on the land here, their existence obliterated by advancing continental ice sheets.

A northern hardwood forest covers Utsayantha and its neighbors. Too low and dry to sustain a spruce-fir forest, striped maple, beech,

The summit of Utsayantha reveals a spectacular view of Stamford and the surrounding area

black cherry, yellow birch, and northern red oak cover the higher elevations. Stands of sugar maple, beech, and yellow birch dominate the lower slopes. Patches of oak and white ash grow in the drier, sunnier habitats. Since farming, logging, and grazing continued into the 1900s, the trees are young.

The Upper Delaware and Schoharie's broad valleys are north and west of these mountains. Towns and farms thrive in these fertile lowlands. The villages of Stamford, Grand Gorge, and Prattsville grew as small market towns among the area's small farms. Hay, wheat, potatoes, and dairy products were the primary agricultural products, and the fields and pastures climbed high into the mountains. Many of these farmlands still reach to the mountains' middle elevations. Settled in the late 18th and early 19th centuries, the towns grew as markets further expanded, and then expanded with the area's logging and leather-tanning industries.

Stamford, named for its mother city in Connecticut, is the region's largest town. Founded in 1796, it grew from a crossroads trading town into a major tourist destination. In its heyday, local promoters billed the town "Queen of the Catskills." The Rexmere, a large hotel of Victorian architecture west of town, is the best surviving example of the Catskills' grand hotels.

By the mid-1800s, timber harvesting became another major component of the local economy. Used for lumber, firewood, tanbark, or barrel-hoop making, trees fueled man's growing economy. Over the past few decades, these depleted forests began the long process of recovery. Oaks, pines, maples, beech, and birch shade the meadows and stone walls. Thousands of slender trees compete for sunlight as open fields revert to forest. Finding and interpreting the area's recent natural history is easy. Although of different species, most trees are similar in size and height, a clue to common origin. A lack of older trees in the forest confirms the land's recent open state.

The late-19th-century economy depleted the region's renewable resources. Jobs vanished as timber ran out and the fields lost fertility. Fire devastated the mountains, while floods ravaged the valleys. Time brought healing to the land, but the economic strength never returned. The late-20th-century economy still needs productive farmland, but it also depends on tourism and recreation. A recovering forest provides the foundation for sustained local growth.

The northwestern Catskills are a soft sculpture of rolling hills, dairy farms, broad valleys, and small towns. They are not rugged mountains, like the Adirondacks, or even the Catskills' higher peaks, but these mountains display their own brand of charm. Their accessibility and history bring a unique regional flavor, while remaining an integral part of the Catskill Mountains.

THE UNTAMED PEAKS

Man-inspired trails do not reach every Catskill summit. Isolated mountain peaks stand covered in wilderness, with nature providing few clues for the uninitiated to follow. No ribbons of packed dirt and bare rock escort visitors to these mountain heights. Confirmation of position does not come with trail junctions and signs. Although it is difficult to visit these unblazed mountaintops, it is certainly possible. Unlike trailed peaks, no set itinerary guides the adventurer. Instead, the art of map and compass, or the more modern Global Positioning Satellites Systems, provide a means to the top. Without a predetermined route, the struggle to climb mountainous terrain becomes an adventure in its own right. Natural processes, not tourism, dominate these remote regions.

State-marked trails ignore half the peaks above 3,500 feet; however, unmaintained trails climb parts of these mountains, so only a few Catskill summits are truly trail-less. Some abandoned paths and logging roads appear on local maps, while others remain known only to a handful of experienced outdoorsmen. The trail-less peaks vary in character. Open summits can make for spirited exploration, while dense vegetation best leaves other peaks to their own company. The choice to visit a peak tests personal growth, wilderness ethic, and tolerance for isolation. Among the Catskill peaks offering this choice are Northdome, Sherill, Vly, Halcott, Rusk, and Southwest Hunter. Most of these neighbor peaks with trails, but nearby roads and stream valleys often provide better access. Only a few of these lonely peaks have significant vistas, but all are rich with wildlife.

Although the Catskills' trail-less summits appear remote, signs and symbols of man's world penetrate even this wilderness. Airplanes cruise the sky, streaking from one civilization center to another. Roads and their constituent cars wind into remote valleys, connecting local communities with distant places. Houses, hamlets, and farms line the roads, a reminder of the mountains' fragile privacy. Views of the surrounding countryside reveal open fields slicing through recovering forests. Broadcast towers pierce the sky and throw their invisible signals around the globe. Man's straight lines provide perspective among nature's random curves. Even in these remote places, litter occasionally mars the ground as an old can, gum wrapper, or soda bottle scars the landscape's natural beauty. The air also shows man's taint, its unhealthy grayish-brown blending sulfur, smoke, and sky. Together, these sights and sounds reduce nature's ability to overwhelm the senses with its millions of randomly-placed trees, rocks, plants, and wildlife.

Wilderness continues to lose its true meaning as civilization expands. While each summit tells a unique story, most features found on these untamed peaks exist elsewhere in the Catskills, and their fragile habitats benefit from man's absence. To realize the importance of preserving these pristine summits, people must understand their value. Good stewardship is essential when visiting these peaks.

🚶 🚶

Northdome Mountain, the Catskills' 29th highest pinnacle, sits west of Westkill Mountain, with a deep glacial notch separating the two peaks. A tangled weave of balsam fir dominates Northdome's 3,610-foot summit. Never logged, this rarely-visited, open and level summit is virgin forest. Although labeled Bluebell Mountain by Arnold Henry Guyot, Northdome remained its official name.

Northdome's ridges reveal many vistas. A good look at the central high peaks opens from the primitive trail climbing its southern face. Equally impressive views grace the rocky, northern slopes. Hunter and Westkill Mountains dwarf Northdome to the north and east. To the south, the central high peaks rise behind Panther Mountain. The Spruceton Valley, Rusk, and the Lexington Range fill the northern foreground.

Sherill Mountain, another difficult peak, is Northdome's western neighbor. Both peaks are in one of the Catskills' deepest wilderness areas. Sherill Mountain is named for Colonel Sherill of the Union army. Owner of a large Shandaken leather tannery, the colonel died a hero at

Gettysburg while holding the center of the line during Pickett's charge. A plaque in his honor stands on the battlefield. A steep, 550-foot notch separates Sherill from its nearest neighbor. No roads or trails lead near it. A mixed fir-hardwood forest caps the 3,540-foot peak.

Southwest Hunter Mountain did not receive attention as a distinct peak until the 1970s. In the Catskills, a named mountaintop must have a 250-foot drop and be a quarter-mile distant from adjoining peaks. This 3,740-foot mountain appears as a spur of Hunter Mountain, but fits the definition for a separate peak. Geographically, it is one of the three peaks composing Hunter Mountain. Few people visit this isolated ridge. On maps, it appears as a 1.5-mile, easy ridgetop walk; however the thick spruce-fir forest makes progress difficult, and finding the top is another challenge. No views open from the summit, but when looking northeast, Hunter's 4,040-foot mass looms through the forest.

Traces of old logging roads lead to Vly Mountain's 3,529-foot summit. A southeast approach to its peak embarks from the col (small gap) between Vly and Bearpen Mountains. Vly displays many signs of past settlement—including farms, pastures, rock walls, old homesites and logging. Man's past activities stripped most of the mountain's forests, but over the past 70 years second-growth forest returned. From man's activities and natural environmental factors, Vly lost its spruce-fir forest. A collection of dwarfed and twisted beech, black cherry, and mountain-ash now clothe the windswept peak. Near the summit, views opens to the northwest and south.

Like most of the northern Catskills, Vly has few distinct features. Heavy glacial erosion softened its contours and eliminated any protruding rock structures. Vly is hard to identify from surrounding territory. As Route 42 enters Deep Clove, it slides by Vly's eastern slopes. The best place to view Vly is east of Prattsville on Route 23A. The open ledges above Pratt's Rocks also provide a good view of Vly Mountain.

Halcott Mountain nestles between Rose and Vly Mountains. It lifts only 20 feet above the 3,500-foot line, and is the second lowest of the Catskill mountains to do so. Halcott's eastern slopes create Deep Clove's western wall. Few people visit Halcott Mountain as no trails lead to the summit, and its nondescript topography provides little guidance. The long, flat ridge culminating as Halcott's peak supports an upper hardwood forest. A few glimpses peek through the tree cover, but no spectacular views open. Belleayre Mountain's ski trails face Halcott and provide a good look at this isolated mountain.

Rusk Mountain rises to 3,680 feet and marks the highest point along the Lexington Range. Located south of Route 23A, it is one peak west of Hunter Mountain. Its southern slopes bound Spruceton Valley. Heavily eroded and smoothed during the ice age, the mountain has few distinct features. Ice-scraped sandstone ledges adorn Rusk's upper elevations. A thick tangle of hobblebush and dwarfed deciduous trees crown its summit, but views open in all directions. Westkill, Northdome, Sherill, and Balsam fill the south and southwest. Huntersfield stands out to the north. The underfit Schoharie Valley fills the northern foreground. Rusk's best views peer east, where Hunter Mountain dominates a scene accented by Kaaterskill High Peak and Roundtop.

Looking east from Rusk—Kaaterskill High Peak, Roundtop, and Hunter Mountains

Named for one of Arnold Henry Guyot's assistants, Samuel Rusk, modern maps place Rusk's summit one peak west of Guyot's position. Guyot often named mountains after his assistants. Peaks throughout the Catskills and the Appalachians bear names he denoted in the 1870s. At that time, most peaks were trail-less, and Guyot often had to climb a tree to determine his position. Although best known for his pioneering work in identifying glacial features, his tireless efforts to measure elevation created his Catskill legacy. Often, his measurements were within 1-2 percent of currently accepted values.

No longer the shunned and isolated mountaintops measured by Guyot, each trail-less peak still can make a quiet retreat. Time and space still separate them from the Catskills' many trails, and all present challenges to surmount. They are places of beauty and serenity, and among the most remote spots in the eastern United States. In contrast with these isolated mountaintops, the busy trails on Overlook and Slide Mountains resemble an interstate highway. The trail-less peaks remain well-hidden from civilization, providing one last refuge and sanctuary for nature's unaltered Catskills.

APPENDIX A: CATSKILL ELEVATIONS

Rank	Mountain	Elevation (feet)
1	Slide	4,180
2	Hunter	4,040
3	Black Dome	3,990
4	Blackhead	3,940
5	Thomas Cole	3,940
6	Westkill	3,880
7	Graham	3,868
8	Doubletop	3,860
9	Cornell	3,860
10	Table	3,847
11	Peekamoose	3,843
12	Plateau	3,840
13	Sugarloaf	3,800
14	Wittenberg	3,780
15	Southwest Hunter	3,740
16	Lone	3,721
17	Balsam Lake	3,720
18	Panther	3,720
19	Big Indian	3,700
20	Friday	3,694
21	Rusk	3,680
22	Kaaterskill High Peak	3,655
23	Twin	3,680
24	Balsam Cap	3,623
25	Fir	3,620
26	Northdome	3,610
27	Balsam	3,600
28	Bearpen	3,600
29	Eagle	3,600
30	Indian Head	3,573
31	Sherill	3,540
32	Vly	3,529
33	Windham High Peak	3,524
34	Halcott	3,520
35	Rocky	3,508

36	Mill Brook Ridge	3,480
37	Dry Brook Ridge	3,460
38	Woodpecker Ridge	3,460
39	Olderbark	3,440
40	Roundtop (by KHP)	3,440
41	Roundtop (by Bearpen)	3,440
42	Huntersfield	3,423
43	Belleayre	3,420

Other Selected Elevations

Place	Elevation
Moresville Range	3,220
Onteora	3,220
Utsayantha	3,214
Giant Ledge	3,200
Burnt Knob	3,180
Overlook	3,150
East Jewett Range	3,140
Plattekill	3,100
High Point	3,098
Tremper	2,740

APPENDIX B: ROUTES DESCRIBED

The Escarpment Wall:
Going North:

Mile   0.0: Begin at Pine Orchard (site of the Catskill Mountain House), head north (blue markers)

0.5: Artist's Rock

1.1: Newman's Ledge, head east on yellow spur trail

1.3: Sunset Rock; retrace route back to Pine Orchard

2.6: Return to Pine Orchard

The Area above Kaaterskill Clove (south of the Catskill Mountain House)

Mile   0.0: Park at southern end of Schutt Road. Carefully cross stream.

0.0: At 3-way trail junction, follow Escarpment Trail west (blue markers)

0.7: Layman Monument; trail bends to the east

1.1: Junction with yellow-blazed trail; continue on Escarpment Trail

1.2: Sunset Rock

1.4: Inspiration Point; turn back

1.7: Junction with yellow-blazed trail; follow it north to Schutt Road Trail (red markers)

2.2: Trail ends at Schutt Road Trail; continue north (bear west)

2.4: Return to 3-way trail junction; cross stream to Schutt Road

Huckleberry Point:

Mile   0.0: State marked snowmobile trail begins at the top of Platte Clove

1.1: Side trail heads east (right) for Huckleberry Point

1.5: Cross Plattekill Creek

1.9: Crest a small rise; begin descent

2.3: Reach Huckleberry Point; go back via same route

4.6: Return to trailhead.

Platte Clove: Not a recommended hike

Kaaterskill High Peak:

Mile   0.0: State-marked snowmobile trail begins at the top of Platte Clove

3.5: Long Path separates and heads for Palenville; remain on snowmobile trail

3.7: Turn south on trail marked with blue paint

4.4: Summit of Kaaterskill High Peak

4.7: Hurricane Ridge

5.1: Junction with snowmobile trail on south side of mountain, begin bushwhack (145-degree bearing)

6.2: Bushwhack ends; return to original trail

6.6: Return to trailhead.

Kaaterskill Clove: (requires 2 vehicles)

Mile   0.0: Pick up stream 1.3 miles west of Palenville just before route 23A crosses to the north bank

0.6: Pass small waterfall as it enters the clove

1.7: Kaaterskill Creek splits; head north (right) along Lake Creek

2.2: Stream rejoins road at Bastion Falls

2.7: Kaaterskill Falls; end of trip (note: State-marked trail ends .1 miles before the falls)

Roundtop: (begin due west of Roundtop along the snowmobile trail—the snowmobile trail can be accessed via the route used to approach Kaaterskill High Peak)

Mile: 0.0: Leave snowmobile trail, begin bushwhack up the mountain

0.4: Reach summit of Roundtop, end of trip

The Devil's Path: (denoted individually)

Indian Head

Mile   0.0: Trail begins at terminus of Prediger Road (red markers)

0.4: Junction with Jimmy Dolan Trail (blue markers)

2.0: Reach Jimmy Dolan Notch and turn east on Devil's Path Trail.

2.5: Pass summit of Indian Head

2.9: Reach excellent viewpoints to eastern (lower) peak

4.5: Devil's Path turns west

5.6: Rejoin the Jimmy Dolan Notch Trail at its lower terminus

6.1: Return to parking area on Prediger Road

Twin

Mile   0.0: Trail begins at terminus of Prediger Road

0.1: Pass sign-in box

0.5: Turn onto Jimmy Dolan Notch Trail (blue markers)

1.6: Trail turns sharply west and begins a steep ascent

2.0: Jimmy Dolan Notch; turn west up Twin (red markers)

2.3: Pass small east-facing ledge

2.4: Open panoramic ledge, summit of lower peak

2.6: Summit of Twin

2.7: West-facing ledge, return by same route

3.4: Return to Jimmy Dolan Notch

5.4: Return to parking area on Prediger Road

Sugarloaf

Mile: 0.0: Trail begins from small parking area along Elka Park Road (yellow markers)

0.3: Trail end; veer east (blue markers)

2.0: Pecoy Notch, turn west (right) to ascend Sugarloaf (red markers)

3.0: Summit of Sugarloaf

3.8: Spur trail leads to open, south-facing ledge, return by same route

4.2: Return to Pecoy Notch

5.9: Trail ends, follow yellow-marked trail

6.2: Return to Elka Park Road

Plateau

Mile: 0.0: Stony Clove (red markers)(2.5 miles south of NY Route 23A on NY Route 214)

0.6: Pass large rock slides

1.0: Orchard Ledge; trail reaches long, level summit

2.6: Summit of Plateau; return by same route

4.2: Return to Orchard Ledge

5.2: Return to Stony Clove

Hunter Mountain:

Mile: 0.0: Begin Becker Hollow Trail along NY Route 214

0.4: Pass concrete dam

2.0: Reach summit ridge, trail ends. Turn north (right).

2.2: Summit clearing, fire tower. Return via same route.

2.4: Return to top of Becker Hollow; turn left

4.4: Return to parking area

The Blackheads: (one-way hike; requires two vehicles)

Mile: 0.0: Start from parking area on Barnum Road (off County Road 40) (red markers)

0.4: Trail bends from southeast to northeast and enters state land

0.9: Viewpoint south located at a switchback

1.5: Summit of Camel's Hump

2.4: Summit of Thomas Cole

3.2: Summit of Black Dome

3.6: Go straight, following the Blackhead Mountain Trail (yellow markers)

4.1: Summit of Blackhead, turn northeast on to escarpment trail (blue markers)

4.8: Turn west (left) at junction with Batavia Kill Trail (yellow markers)

6.1: Reach parking area at end of Black Dome Valley Road

Windham High Peak:

Mile: 0.0: Trail (red markers) begins at parking area on Big Hollow Road; head north

1.1: Trail ends at Escarpment Trail (blue markers); Turn west (left)

2.4: Trail reaches highest point along Burnt Knob

3.0: Notch between Burnt Knob and Windham

3.8: Summit of Windham. Views from both sides of the summit. Return via same route.

6.5: Turn south back into Black Dome Valley

7.6: Return to parking area on Big Hollow Road

Westkill Mountain:

Mile: 0.0: Trail begins at end of Spruceton Road (blue markers)

1.0: Diamond Notch Falls. Trail crosses bridge. Turn west (red markers) toward Westkill's summit.

2.4: Pass small rock cave.

3.1: Buck Ridge Lookout

3.2: Pass ledge with a northern overlook

3.3: Summit of Westkill. Return via same route.

5.6: Trail junction at Diamond Notch Falls

6.6: Return to Spruceton Road parking area

Bearpen Mountain: (unmarked trail follows an old dirt road)

Mile: 0.0: Trail begins along Greene County Route 2 (accessible from NY Route 23A)

3.0: Pass small pond

3.2: Reach top of old ski slopes

3.3: Summit of Bearpen, return by same route

6.6: Return to parking area

Pratt's Rocks:

Mile: 0.0: Begin at parking area along NY Route 23

            0.2: Reach Pratt's Rocks, continue east along ridgeline trail

            0.4: Reach open ledges, return by same route

            0.8: Return to parking area

The Northwestern Catskills: (most are trail-less)

Utsayantha (a dirt road open to vehicle traffic)

Mile: 0.0: Follow Mountain Avenue (off NY Route 23) to dirt road ascending Utsayantha

            1.2: Summit of Utsayantha

YES, I'd like to order:

Book Two of *Catskill Trails: The Southern Catskills*.
Enclosed is my check, or credit card payment information.

No. of copies	Price	Total
	@ $14.95	
	Plus shipping ($2.50 for 1st book $.50 each additional)	
	NYS residents add 8% sales tax	
	TOTAL	

Name _____

Address _____

City _____

State _____ Zip _____

Telephone _____

<u>Credit Card Customers</u>

Signature _____

Visa or MC # _____

Exp. Date _____

Telephone # _____

<u>Mail this coupon with check enclosed to:</u>
Black Dome Press, 1011 Route 296, Hensonville, NY 12439.
Credit card customers may mail or fax to 518-734-5802
or call to order 800-513-9013

ABOUT THE AUTHOR

Ed Henry grew up in the Catskill Mountains, just outside of Woodstock. He has been exploring and writing about the Appalachian Mountains and surrounding regions for the past twenty-five years.

Besides his adventures in the Catskills and the nearby Shawangunk Mountains, Henry has worked for the U.S. Forest Service and as a park ranger in the Shenandoah and Great Smoky Mountains National Parks. He now works for the U.S. Fish and Wildlife Service and is the Refuge Manager for the Wallkill River and Shawangunk Grasslands National Wildlife Refuges.

Henry is the author of two other books, *Catskill Trails: A Ranger's Guide to the High Peaks, Book II, The Central Catskills* (Black Dome Press, 2000) and *Gunks Trails: A Ranger's Guide to the Shawangunk Mountains* (Black Dome Press, 2003) plus numerous magazine articles. His fourth book, a guide to the Taconic and Berkshire mountains, is scheduled to be published by Black Dome Press in 2007.

Henry has a master's degree in forest ecology from SUNY's College of Environmental Science and Forestry in Syracuse, New York. He presently lives in Wurtsboro, New York.

Catskill Forest Preserve

181

Catskill Map, copyright © NYS DEC, used by permission.